BEGINNINGS:

Seeking God's Kingdom In the Midst of Trials and Temptations

A Self-Counsel Journal for Women by

Alex Kocher and Brenda Payne

Beginnings:
Seeking God's Kingdom in the Midst of Trials and Temptations

Alex and Brenda welcome your feedback and can be contacted at:
https://www.knownministries.org/about-us/contact/

First Printing, 2019

ISBN 13: 978-1-73323-440-5

Cover artwork and design by Lauren Duncan and Noah Craig

Editing and typesetting by Rick Steele Editorial Services
(https://steeleeditorialservices.myportfolio.com) with help from Noah Craig, Dunlap, TN

Printed in the United States of America

To our daughters and mothers, both physical and spiritual.
May we seek His kingdom and His righteousness first in our hearts and lives!

Introduction

As biblical counselors, we primarily meet with Christian women. Many of these women have studied the Bible but are unsure how to connect the Word of God to their daily thinking and living. As a result, they are unable to connect the truth with their sin and suffering struggles. This study emphasizes a need for solid doctrine (belief) and application (practice) of God's Word. We pray this process of learning doctrine and applying it in a self-counsel journal to your own trials and temptation will bring about personal transformation in your life. Then, when you finish the last page of the book, we hope you will flip it over and study it again with another woman. That is how the one-another revolution continues in the hearts and lives of believers, and that is how the kingdom of God moves ahead here on earth.

Each day, you encounter trials and temptations that entice you to pledge your allegiance to a rule and a kingdom other than God's. Jesus ends his discourse on worry with a reminder to, "seek first the kingdom of God and His righteousness," (Matt. 6:33) because He knows that the cares of this world make it so easy for us to forget what is of utmost importance, the kingdom of God. So, what is the kingdom of God? It is the rule and reign of the King, but it is not primarily a place. The kingdom is wherever Jesus is. Where is Jesus today? He is in heaven, but He also lives in each of His followers through the person of the Holy Spirit. Jesus constantly talked about the kingdom of God, and His life exemplified the rule and reign of God on earth. When He went back to the Father, He left us, His followers, with a commission to represent Him and to see His kingdom here on earth until He comes again to establish His kingdom forever.

The world will not be won through political, educational, or social reforms because none of these are God's appointed means to build His kingdom on earth. That responsibility belongs to the church. Bringing His kingdom here to earth will require a revolution—a true upheaval of our natural way of thinking and doing. That "one-another revolution" starts with you! This revolution is made up of women who apply God's word to their own lives and then help others do the same. Make no mistake, many forces in the culture are committed to defying God and His rule in every aspect of life. You must commit to the most important work of the faith: cooperating with God for personal transformation into Christ-likeness and then leading other women to trust and obey Jesus for the glory of the King.

Genesis 1—3 is the primary text for this work. Please read these three chapters regularly as you work through this study. They are vital to understanding the kingdom of God and our place in it. The importance of prayer cannot be overstated. This study is only a tool for change, God alone brings about change that is pleasing to Him. Please use this material prayerfully, asking God to change you and make you a conduit of change for others. In this study, we hope to achieve three goals:

1. To help you evaluate your life in light of the King and His kingdom
2. To guide you through a self-counsel journal that will test what you think and believe in light of the Word of God and will reorient you to the King and His kingdom in times of trial and temptation
3. To equip you to help others as you seek to point them to the King and His kingdom (You will only be able to help others when you can do this for yourself.)

Study Snapshot

Questions within Each Chapter: Each chapter is designed to present doctrinal truths in simple and understandable ways. You are actually getting a lesson on the theology of God and the theology of man! There are thought provoking questions incorporated in each chapter which we hope will help you remember and wrestle with the truths.

The Kingdom Life Chapter Review: At the end of each chapter, you will find a question to slow you down as you consider the doctrine that has been presented. To cement these concepts in your mind, take some time to meditate on what you learned and put it in writing. This will also help equip you as you work through your self-counsel journals.

Self-Counsel Journal: At the end of each chapter you will read Diane's story and see how she uses the self-counsel journal questions in her own life. Then, you will be able to use these same questions and apply them to a trial or temptation in your life. Use this journal regularly (even daily) as a way to reorient yourself to the King and His kingdom and to align your life with His loving rule. You may be tempted to skip this part of the study, but please don't. The self-counsel journal is vital to gaining the full benefit of this study.

Self-Counsel Journal Sample Instructions:

Group Discussion Questions: Change is community project! When God saved you, He saved you to be part of His family. Even though you will benefit by doing this study solo, the greatest benefit will come when you learn with others. Grab at least one other friend. Meet with your friend(s) to discuss your journaling and work through these additional questions.

Chapter Summaries

Here is a summary of each chapter. Each week begins with a study focused on sound doctrine and culminates with the self-counsel journal application.

Chapter 1 Rule: God as King. Women are created by God to live in His kingdom and under His rule. When you forget that God is King, you lose sight of the big story of Scripture, the kingdom of God. As a result, you live for your own kingdom and under your own rule.

Chapter 2 Relate: God as Father. As your loving Father, God has provided for you to be in relationship with Him through Jesus. When you forget that God is your Father, you will live as a slave to sin or be defined by your suffering. When you remember that God is your loving Father, you will live as a beloved daughter who honors God and serves others as Jesus did.

Chapter 3 Reflect: Made in His Image. Women are made in the image of God, but sin marred that image. As a believer, the image of God is being renewed in you through a relationship with Jesus Christ. When you fail to recognize that you are an image-bearer, you won't accurately reflect Him in every sphere of your life. When you recognize what it means to be an image-bearer, you will relate to others well and rightly represent Him.

Chapter 4 Represent: Made by His Design. God made women as helpers to uniquely magnify His glory. When you don't embrace and operate according to your particular design, you war against your King and not for Him. As an "essential ally," you are designed to fill the gaps in the spheres where God has placed you.

Chapter 5 Reproduce: Made to Multiply. God desires to fill the earth with worshipers who glorify Him as the ultimate king. He created you to be a worshiper and commissioned you to lead others to worship Him. Remembering your mission helps you build relationships that are intentional and purposeful for the kingdom.

Chapter 6 Restore: Made to Beautify. Women are called to partner with God to bring order from chaos and to preserve that improved condition. Failing to understand this aspect of your mission makes you ineffective and unproductive. Understanding the term "beautify" helps you to find meaning and purpose in the everyday tasks of life.

Chapter 7 Repeat: The Mission. Women have a special mandate to teach the next generation of women and model what it means to be a daughter of the King. Failing to fulfill this mandate is a missed opportunity to cooperate with God in His Great Commission ("Great" because it is so vast but also because it is the most excellent mission to which we can give our lives). Let's remember, only two things will last: the souls of men and the Word of God.

Rule   Relate   Reflect   Represent   Reproduce   Restore   Repeat

Contents

CHAPTER 1
RULE: GOD AS KING

1. Read the chapter and prayerfully answer the questions throughout the study to consider the truth of God's Rule as King.

2. Use the Kingdom Life Chapter Review to reflect on the doctrinal truths that are new or reinforced.

3. Use the Self-Counsel Journal to apply God's RULE to your heart and life. Do as many journal entries as you have need and time. You can copy the journal page or print more journal pages at the website. (See the journal instructions in the Journal Introduction and the sample Self Counsel Journal, Diane's Story, for help. For additional help and examples go to knownministries.org.)

4. If you are meeting with a friend(s), use the Group Discussion Questions in Appendix II.

CHAPTER ONE

RULE: GOD AS KING

Scripture: Genesis 1–3

"Lord Almighty, the God of Israel, enthroned between the cherubim, you alone are God over all the kingdoms of the earth. You have made heaven and earth." (Isaiah 37:16)

The True Story of the World

"In the beginning, God . . ." You will recognize those opening words from the story of the Bible. Calling the Bible a story does not suggest that it is like any other book or that it is a good fiction read. God inspired the Bible, without error, and it is the truest story ever written. Saying the Bible is a story means it is a narrative with characters, themes, and a plot that revolve around a central subject: the King and His kingdom. Author Graeme Goldsworthy defines God's kingdom as, "God's people, in God's place, under God's rule."

How do you typically read the Bible? Look at the list below, and check the ways you view or use the Bible:

_____ self-help book _____ book of comfort _____ instruction manual
_____ history book _____ wisdom sayings _____ series of short stories
_____ great literature _____ prophecy _____ family heirloom

The Bible is certainly all of the above; however, it is far more. If you miss the big picture of the Bible you may miss knowing the King and understanding your place in His Kingdom.

The Story of the King

"In the beginning, God" means that God is the starting place of the story. In reality, He existed before this story even began, because He alone has no beginning and no end (Rev. 1:8). God, the Eternal King, is the central character of the story. The King acts throughout the story to establish and maintain His kingdom. You may be wondering who made God the King? God did! As the Creator of all things, He alone deserves the title of King of all the earth (Ps. 47). God not only has the *right* to be king, He is the only One *qualified* to be King of Kings. He alone is the Holy One. This means God alone exists in absolute perfection and is completely set apart from His creation. God has many attributes human beings do not possess, and the attributes He shares with humanity (like love, joy, and peace) He possesses to the highest degree possible. He is THE MOST of everything He is: THE MOST loving, THE MOST powerful, THE MOST wise, etc.

In addition, only God can achieve perfection in all His attributes without contradicting Himself. In other words, He is completely loving in His justice and completely just in His love. God's perfection sets Him so far apart from mankind that many people refer to God's holiness as His "otherness." Since He is so separate from creation, you cannot completely comprehend Him. Yet, He chooses to draw near to you, creating a kingdom where He rules His people in love. What an amazing thought, the King of Kings longs to come close to know you and love you! While you cannot comprehend all of Him, the King still reveals Himself in love to you through His creation, His Son, and His Word.

In the sixth chapter of Isaiah, the prophet had a vision of the Lord sitting on His throne. He heard the angels singing the praises of the God saying, "Holy, holy, holy is the LORD of hosts; the whole earth is full of his glory!" (Is 6:3). Then, "the foundations of the thresholds shook at the voice of him who called, and the house was filled with smoke" (Isa. 6:4). And Isaiah said: "Woe is me! For I am lost; for I am a man of unclean lips, and I dwell in the midst of a people of unclean lips; for my eyes have seen the King, the LORD of hosts!" (Isa. 6:5).

God's holiness caused Isaiah to recognize his own unworthiness and be in awe of God. In your own words, write out what Isaiah's reaction was to the holiness of God.

Have you ever had an experience of the presence of God that left you feeling in awe of the Lord or unworthy before Him? Describe it below.

The King Creates a Place and a People

The story continues, "In the beginning God created." Our King spoke and brought the heavens and the earth into existence. He alone is the true creator who created the world out of nothing. All other creating that mankind does comes from His creation. He created the world and all that is in it by the power of His Word. As God spoke, He initiated His kingdom into a particular place, the Garden of Eden. For the purpose of His glory and pleasure, God filled the earth with water, sun, moon, stars, plants, animals, and finally, people. He called His creation good.

Our King not only created the place for His kingdom, He fashioned a people for His Kingdom. God had no need for people. Throughout eternity, the Godhead (the Father, Son, and Holy Spirit), enjoyed perfect unity, fellowship, and satisfaction. Yet, God spoke Adam and Eve into existence to bring pleasure and glory to Himself. When He created the earth and all its creatures, He sat back and called it good. However, it was only after He created man and woman when He declared all He made *"very good"* (Gen. 1:31). Arranging flowers, cooking food, making music, are all wonderful endeavors, but they pale in comparison to the joy of seeing a human being born! If you have experienced childbirth or rejoiced with someone who has given birth, you might catch a glimpse of God's good pleasure in creating mankind.

> **O**ur Creator fashioned mankind and then draws near and cares for His creation.

God is not a creator who made us and then removed Himself from us. He created us for relationship with Himself and with others. He made us distinct from the rest of His creation, breathing His breath into the living soul of man (Gen. 2:7). He stamped us with His image to represent Him, and He made us to relate to Him in a way that was unlike the rest of creation. The King came near to Adam and Eve. He walked and talked in the garden and enjoyed intimate fellowship with them. If you read the stories of Greek and Roman mythology, you see gods who treat humans disdainfully for their own selfish whims and well-being. Our Creator fashioned mankind and then draws near and cares for His creation! This is astonishing! When the psalmist considered that the King who created the world would stoop to be in relationship with him, he exclaimed, "*When I look at your heavens, the work of your fingers, the moon and the stars, which you have set in place, what is man that you are mindful of him, and the son of man that you care for him?*" (Ps. 8:3–4, ESV).

Have you ever marveled at a spider web, a sunrise, or sunset, or some other part of God's creation that caused you to worship the creativity and intelligence of your King? When you consider all of God's creation, it's humbling that He chose to draw near to and care for you. Take some time today to study creation and let yourself be in awe. Reflect on that time below.

The King's Rule

As Creator, God has the unquestionable and absolute right to rule as King. This is known as Sovereignty. As the King, He alone possesses the ultimate power over His kingdom. He rules over all the rulers of the earth. One of the great kings of the Old Testament, David, recognized that God was the ruler over all, "*Lord, the God of our ancestors, are you not the God who is in heaven? You rule over all the kingdoms of the nations. Power and might are in your hand, and no one can withstand you*" (2 Chron. 20:6, NIV). When God placed Adam and Eve in the Garden, they were His children living under His loving rule. Unlike human authority, which is so easily corrupted, God's authority over you is always loving, because God is love (1 John 4:16). If you are His child, all His laws and commands are for your good. God simply knows that your greatest fulfillment and joy come from living by faith in obedience to Him.

The greatest threat to God's rule in your life is your desire for autonomy, or self-rule. When you forget that you live in God's kingdom under God's rule, you begin to live for your own kingdom and rule. Each of you has places where God has given you authority. This can be any place that you hold decision-making power (school, work, car, home, relationships). Write out the areas/places where God has given you rule. Pick one area and consider how God has helped you to exercise authority and bring a little bit of His kingdom rule to earth.

Rebellion against the King

God's people, in God's place, under God's rule, quickly came under attack. God gave Adam and Eve everything in His creation to enjoy. Most importantly, He gave them full and free access to Himself. As long as Adam and Eve obeyed His loving rule, they would enjoy both forever. However, there was one prohibition in the garden; one thing God said not to do. God told Adam and Eve not to eat from one tree, *". . . but of the tree of the knowledge of good and evil you shall not eat, for in the day that you eat of it you shall surely die"* (Gen. 2:17). God gave Adam and Eve this rule for their own protection! They did not know the terrible reality of evil. Lurking in the King's garden was an intruder, Satan. The Bible indicates Satan was originally one of God's holy angels. He became proud and jealous of God and mounted an insurrection in the heavenly realms. His rebellion was quickly squelched, and he was cast out of heaven along with his army of fallen angels (Is. 14:12-15). But Satan is relentless. He tried to usurp the throne again. Here is the biblical account:

> *Now the serpent was more crafty than any other beast of the field that the **Lord** God had made. He said to the woman, "Did God actually say, 'You shall not eat of any tree in the garden'?" And the woman said to the serpent,*

"We may eat of the fruit of the trees in the garden, but God said, 'You shall not eat of the fruit of the tree that is in the midst of the garden, neither shall you touch it, lest you die.'" But the serpent said to the woman, "You will not surely die. For God knows that when you eat of it your eyes will be opened, and you will be like God, knowing good and evil." So when the woman saw that the tree was good for food, and that it was a delight to the eyes, and that the tree was to be desired to make one wise, she took of its fruit and ate, and she also gave some to her husband who was with her, and he ate. Then the eyes of both were opened, and they knew that they were naked. And they sewed fig leaves together and made themselves loincloths. (Gen. 3:1–7)

In this attack on God's rule, Satan sought to undermine God's authority by attacking His Word, which is the revelation of His character and promises. By maligning God's Word, Satan tempted Adam and Eve to question God's love for them and God's right to rule over them. The Apostle Paul warned the Corinthian church to be aware of the devil's schemes (2 Cor. 2:11). He told the Ephesians to put on the full armor of God, **"so that you can take your stand against the devil's schemes"** (Eph. 6:11). The disciple, Peter, warned, **"Be sober-minded; be watchful. Your adversary the devil prowls around like a roaring lion, seeking someone to devour"** (1 Pet. 5:8). Remember that your enemy is shrewd and subtle. Study his tactics so that you know how to fight his lies and hold fast to the truth of God's Word. Here's how he often works:

First, Satan seduced Eve to doubt God with a simple question **"Did God actually say, 'You shall not eat of any tree in the garden?'"** (emphasis added). Satan made God's rule seem unreasonable, restrictive, and unloving. He wanted Eve to focus on what she did not have instead of the bounty that God had given her. When you struggle with sin or suffering, Satan wants you to doubt God's Word and His character so you will cast off His rule in your life.

Second, Satan minimized the consequences of sin. He assured Eve, **"You will not surely die."** When you struggle with sin or suffering, Satan wants to remove the fear of disobedience by convincing you the consequences will be minimal or nonexistent.

Third, Satan impugned God's motive. *"God knows that when you eat of it your eyes will be opened, and you will be like God, knowing good and evil."* In your sin and suffering, Satan wants you to believe God is withholding something good from you and does not have your best interests or protection at heart.

Finally, Satan appealed to Eve's autonomy, *"You will be like God."* In your sin and suffering, Satan wants to convince you to be your own king under your own rule. He wants you to believe that you can trust yourself more than you can trust God.

> Think about how Satan has used these tactics to tempt you to sin:
>
> How has Satan tempted you to doubt God's Word or maligned it?
>
> How has Satan tempted you to believe consequences would be marginal or nonexistent?
>
> How has Satan tempted you to believe God was withholding something good from you or not protecting you?
>
> How has Satan tempted you to be your own ruler, leading you to believe you can trust yourself better than you can trust God?
>
> In contrast, can you describe a time when you made a hard choice to obey God?

It looked like the kingdom had been lost. It appeared the enemy had won, and the King had been dethroned. Satan must have gloated over his seeming victory. Adam and Eve exchanged the truth of God for a lie and the entire universe was plunged into complete and utter disaster. Sin, rebellion against God's rule, entered into the world and created a catastrophe of cosmic proportions. All creation plunged into a new paradigm of decay and death which is called "The Fall." In addition, God pronounced judgment on Adam and Eve for their rebellion. This judgment, which extended to all of creation is known as "The Curse." Four key relationships were devastated:

A person's relationship with God
A person's relationship with himself/herself
A person's relationship with others
A person's relationship with the creation

Adam and Eve immediately sensed their intimacy with the King was lost. Their eyes were opened to evil. Think about the shocking nature of this new reality. You might compare it to the reaction of a young child to an R-rated horror film. Adam and Eve became aware of their nakedness and vulnerability. The world they knew had been turned upside down. In their guilt and shame, they were terrified and hid from God. Then they turned on each other, blaming one another for being disobedient. Where love once reigned, pride and selfishness now ruled the hearts of Adam and Eve.

As a result of this fall into sin, God pronounced a judgment which promised even more hardship. For Adam and all men thereafter, work would be difficult and often futile. For Eve and all future women, childbirth and child rearing would bring pain. In addition, the marriage relationship would no longer be the loving intimacy Adam and Eve enjoyed in the Garden. Spouses would be engaged in a constant power struggle (Gen. 3:16-19). Rebellion became mankind's natural position against God and the normal expression of life. The people God created like Him in true righteousness and holiness (Eph. 4:24) became His enemies (Rom. 5:10; Col. 1:21). All creation groans under the curse of decay and death (Rom. 8:19-23). Nothing and no one are left untouched by the curse.

However, the King in His mercy did not kill Adam and Eve immediately, because He had a much bigger plan. Adam and Eve's rebellion did not take God by surprise. The story was unfolding according to His plan. Indeed, if the sin of Adam and Eve occurred outside of God's plan, it would make them more powerful than the King. Theologian R.C Sproul, says, "If there is one maverick molecule in all the universe, then God is not sovereign. And if God is not sovereign, He is not God." The sovereign King was still firmly on His throne (Ps. 22:28). The story is not over, in fact, the best part is yet to come!

When you see evil in our world and experience difficulty in your own life, it can be troublesome to understand why God would allow such things. Just because God allows evil does not make Him the author of evil (James 1:13). Author Joni Eareckson Tada has spent the last fifty years as a quadriplegic due to a diving accident she had as a teenager. Even in the midst of daily suffering, she recognizes that "God allows what He hates, to accomplish what He loves." Sin and suffering often feel difficult and beyond what you can bear because they are too heavy for you to bear alone. Nothing is too heavy for your King. He upholds the world in the palm of His hand, and He will carry you in your struggles. Although you may not know why difficult things happen now, you can trust that ultimately, He loves you, and His rule over you is good (Rom. 8:28-29).

> The Bible shows you from beginning to end that the King is for you. Yet, since the Fall, many believe that God does not have their best interests at heart. Can you think of a specific area where you are finding it difficult to trust God? How would you live differently today if you believed that God is FOR you?

The Returning King

The King was present in His place, His kingdom. Adam and Eve walked and talked with the King in the beauty of His creation. However, in God's Kingdom "very good" quickly turned to "very bad." Although they experienced perfect fellowship with the King, Adam and Eve rebelled against His rule by breaking His law. Adam and Eve desired to live under their own rule more than the King's. This perfect kingdom was lost by the man and woman's disobedience to their King. But thankfully, that is not the end of the story. God planned for this revolt, and in His mercy, He provided a way, in Christ, for His people to once again be under His loving rule. The kingdom of God now resides in His people who have placed their trust in Him. As a believer, you fight to bring God's rule of love to earth, and you long for the restoration of the presence of the King in a particular place once again. One day King Jesus will come again to live among His people in a new garden, the new heavens and new earth (Rev. 21:1). People from every tribe and tongue and nation will worship Him together. He will once and for all put His enemies under His feet, and He will reign as King forever and ever.

> As a believer, you fight to bring God's rule of love to earth, and you long for the restoration of the presence of the King in a particular place once again.

"THE KINGDOM LIFE" CHAPTER REVIEW

What doctrinal concepts were new or reinforced for you in this section?

SELF-COUNSEL JOURNAL

Read the Journal Instructions and the Journal Samples for help. (You can also find additional help and blank journal pages at knownministries.org.)

Complete the Self-Counsel Journal to connect your current struggle to God's RULE as King this week.

Self-Counsel Journal Instructions (More on p. 94)

Did you know you counsel yourself all day, every day? Typically, these conversations occur in your mind. You interpret life and make decisions about what you will believe, whom you will trust, and how you will respond. What we have found in working with hundreds of women is that often this self-counsel is void of God and His wisdom. It is one thing to know God is love, but it is a completely different matter to counsel yourself according to His love when trouble arises. As you talk to yourself in the secret space of your own heart you have the opportunity to direct your thinking according to God and His Word. It is here in the heart where desires and values are wrestled down. It is here that you can acknowledge God's love and submit to His reign in your daily life. What type of counselor are you? Do you point yourself back to the realities of the King and His kingdom? This journal will lead you through biblical self-counsel that will enable you not to just store up more knowledge but to apply that knowledge. Application begins as you are transformed by the renewing of your mind, remembering who God is, what He has done for you in Christ, and what He requires of you as His beloved daughter.

God uses our struggles to produce humility and dependence on Him that will bring about trust and obedience. This study is just one of many ways to help you see God's love *for* you and His loving rule *over* you. The more you practice self-counsel, the more it will become a normal part of your thinking and help you "seek first His kingdom" in every area of life. Furthermore, as your thinking is increasingly guided by a Scripture, it will lead to more biblical living and you will be better equipped to help others. Please take the time to answer the questions in writing. We know writing things down takes time, yet somehow writing things down brings new insight and reinforces right thinking.

There are no shortcuts to the "one another revolution": you cannot change or help someone else change if you don't commit the time necessary. We dare you! Once you have become accustomed to working through the journals in writing, you will be able to more quickly work through them in your head by using the 6 R's. You will have disciplined yourself for godliness through repeated training and developed some strong spiritual muscles (1 Tim. 4:8; Heb. 12:11).

To help you see the Self-Counsel Journal in action, we have included a sample SELF-COUNSEL JOURNAL: DIANE'S STORY. Diane uses the SAME trial for each chapter's questions. In Self-Counsel Journal Instructions on page 94, we have Lana's story to provide additional information on how to use the Self-Counsel Journal. Please notice that in every journaling response there are at least six components:

Honesty. God really cares about your struggles. Run to Him and pour out your heart before Him.

Confession. Look at what you wrote down. Ask the Holy Spirit to show you where your thinking and believing are wrong or your hoping and trusting is misplaced. Simply confess it as sin and ask for forgiveness.

Thankfulness. God is always working on your behalf. Take inventory of your spiritual blessings and thank Him.

Repentance. Repent just means to turn from your sin and turn to God in faith and obedience. You cannot change apart from the Holy Spirit who gives you the desire and power to change. Take hold of Him by faith and cling to Him for real and lasting change that pleases God.

Petition. Ask God for help. You may want to write your journal entries directly to God. He is listening and ready to help you.

Repetition. You are only seeing one journal entry on one specific struggle. You can use this journal over and over again as you go deeper into one struggle or as you encounter other trials. The book of James says that perseverance is necessary for spiritual growth (James 1:2-4). Don't give up! The journal is a meditation tool to see more of His glorious grace through the prism of your problems.

RULE
Self-Counsel Journal Sample

This Self-Counsel Journal is written by a real person to help you understand how to use the journals. The journal questions are written in bold. *The response is written in italics.*

SAMPLE: DIANE'S STORY

Write out current events or insights in the struggle you have chosen:

After several years in a very difficult job, my husband, Ron, has suddenly taken a new job in a different city which will require our family to move. We are in the early stages of renovating an old house that we will have to finish before we can sell it and move. In the meantime, Ron spends four nights each week in the city where his job is and comes home on weekends. He loves his job but not the commuting. While I am absolutely sure that this is the Lord's will and provision for us, I do not want to move. My children have grown up here. Many of our friends are here. I love my church, I love my neighbors, I love my old house, and I love my children's school. I have two children still living at home—one who is a junior in high school and also does not want to move. Even though I don't want to move, I can see tangible ways that the Lord has been preparing me for this, but I still don't want to go. As a child, I moved fourteen times and attended six different schools. I have made a heart idol out of having roots in a community.

What are you thinking? Put your internal monologue in quotations exactly how you talk to yourself. This step allows you to see the orientation of your heart and reveals your current self-counsel.

"Ugh! I hate change!" "It's so expensive to live there. How will we be able to afford it?" "The houses there are all ugly and expensive" "Why couldn't he just suck it up and stay at his job here?" "Why couldn't he take a different job here in town?" "I don't want to find a new house or church or friends. I like what I have here." "It's really unfair to uproot our family, especially our daughter who has been in the same school with the same friends for twelve years."

Rule — Relate — Reflect — Represent — Reproduce — Restore — Repeat

RULE
Self-Counsel Journal
Sample: Diane's Story

Now that you understand Diane's struggle, let's see how she applies the concept of God as King to this struggle with moving.

Rule: God as King—Am I living under the absolute rule of the Most High King of the Universe in my heart and life?

No, if I were living under His absolute rule, I would trust His plans for my life. Instead my anxiety shows that I want control and don't trust His love for me.

Who or what is ruling my heart? (Whoever or whatever rules you controls you.) Who or what is competing for God's rule in my life?

My desire for control; my desire for security; my desire for comfort for myself and my daughter; my desire for lack of conflict with my daughter; fear of the unknown.

Am I challenging God's right to rule in my life? How can I counsel myself to trust His rule?

Ouch! Without realizing it, I am challenging His right to rule. I must remind myself of Who He is and that He has the absolute right to rule over my life—not me. I need the constant reminder that He is God and I am not. I need to regularly remind myself of His attributes of sovereignty, goodness, love, faithfulness, omnipotence

How does God's holiness (the perfection of all His attributes) comfort me? What attribute of God is especially meaningful for me now? What would change if I embraced this attribute?

Because He is sovereign, He has the absolute right to rule my life. Because He is omnipotent, omniscient, omnipresent, etc., He has the ability to rule my life. But I am comforted because of His goodness, love, faithfulness, I can trust Him to act in ways that are for my good and His glory.

How does the sovereignty of God (His absolute rule over the universe) comfort me? How does it trouble me? How should it challenge my current thinking?

It comforts me only when I remember that because of His attributes, He is uniquely and only qualified to rule. He is able, but He is also invested in me. He has purchased me with the sacrificial blood of His Son. Who am I to think that I know better or to doubt His love for me?

How is Satan undermining God's rule in my life by attacking the truths of God's Word and His character?

Satan tells me the same lie that he told Eve in the garden. I question His love for me. I doubt that He is acting for my good. Satan also tempts me to pridefully believe that I have a better grasp on what's best for family than God does.

How does the hope of God's future reign help me in my current circumstances?

The hope of God's future reign reminds me that my sinful power struggle for control will one day end, but in the meantime, I must continue to fight to submit my sinful heart to His reign and rule.

RULE
Self-Counsel Journal

Write out events or insights in a current struggle you are enduring:

What are you thinking? Put your internal monologue in quotations exactly how you talk to yourself. This step allows you to see the orientation of your heart and reveals your current self-counsel.

How are you responding? (Include actions, words, feelings, and attitudes.)

Rule: God as King—*Am I living under the absolute rule of the most high King of the Universe in my heart and life?*

1. Who or what is ruling my heart? (Whoever or whatever rules you controls you.) Who or what is competing for God's rule in my life?

2. Am I challenging God's right to rule in my life? How can I counsel myself to trust His rule?

3. How does God's holiness (the perfection of all His attributes) comfort me? What attribute of God is especially meaningful for me now? What would change if I embraced this attribute?

4. How does the sovereignty of God (His absolute rule over the universe) comfort me? How does it trouble me? How should it challenge my current thinking?

5. How is Satan undermining God's rule in my life by attacking the truths of God's Word and His character?

6. How does the hope of God's future reign help me in my current circumstances?

NOTES

Rule   Relate   Reflect   Represent   Reproduce   Restore   Repeat

CHAPTER 2
RELATE: GOD AS FATHER

1. Read the chapter and prayerfully answer the questions throughout the study to consider the truth of Relating to God as Father.

2. Use the Kingdom Life Chapter Review to reflect on the doctrinal truths that are new or reinforced.

3. Use the Self-Counsel Journal to continue to write about God's RULE in your life. Now add RELATE to each journal entry. Do as many journal entries as you have need and time. You can copy the journal pages or print more at the website. (See the journal instructions in the Journal Introduction and the sample Self Counsel Journal, Diane's Story, for help. For additional help and examples go to knownministries.org.)

4. If you are meeting with a friend(s), use the Group Discussion Questions in Appendix II.

CHAPTER TWO

RELATE: GOD AS FATHER

Scripture: Genesis 1–3; Matthew 26–28

As a father shows compassion to his children, so the LORD shows compassion to those who fear him (Ps. 103:13).

See what kind of love the Father has given to us, that we should be called children of God; and so we are. The reason why the world does not know us is that it did not know him. (1 John 3:1).

In the last chapter, it looked like God's kingdom might be coming to an end. The King's people, Adam and Eve, rebelled against His rule and had to be banned from His place, the Garden. Why would a God with ultimate power not just wipe out Adam and Eve and start over with a people who obeyed Him? You see, it was God's plan all along to show the fullness of His glory by purchasing back His people and all of creation from the clutches of sin and put them back in a right relationship with Him.

God was not shocked by Adam and Eve's sin. Before the world began, He planned the great rescue mission of His people and the restoration of His kingdom. However, in His holiness, He could not tolerate man's sin. God's holiness means He is in a class all by Himself; but it also means He is completely, morally pure. He is light, and in Him there is no darkness (1 John 1:5). Adam and Eve were removed from the Garden because sin separates mankind from God. If they were going to find their way back to the Father, someone would have to do what Adam and Eve could not do—live a perfect life and pay the punishment of death in their place.

Even as the holy King was ushering Adam and Eve out of the Garden, He was acting as the loving Father making provision for them to return to Him and become His children. In Genesis 3:15, God makes the first promise that He would conquer Satan and ultimately bring His children home to Him. He demonstrates that promise by sacrificing an animal to physically clothe Adam and Eve. The animal's blood was shed to physically cover Adam and Eve, and it pointed to Jesus' blood that was shed to cover the sin of all of His children.

King as Father

When you think of God as King, you might picture a dignified and serious ruler who sits on an elevated throne surrounded by wealth and honor. How does this picture change if this king is also your father? You would know and experience him in a completely different way. You would have access to him that others don't have. You would have rights and privileges that others don't enjoy. You would even have certain responsibilities. The imagery may be lost on you if you have never experienced a monarchy. However, you may remember that some of the most iconic pictures from 1963 were of John F. Kennedy Jr. playing in the Oval Office of his father, President Kennedy. JFK Jr. not only knew the leader of the free world, but he had intimate access to him, crouching under his desk, playing hide-and-seek, and sitting on his lap. Yes, his father was one of the most powerful men in the world, but for JFK Jr., he was just his daddy.

> God wants to show you the love of the true Father who loves you with an everlasting and perfect love.

For some of you, the idea of a father is not a pleasant or loving one. Maybe your earthly father or other father figure was harsh, abusive, or neglectful, leaving you with deep hurts and bad memories. You may feel distrustful of men or authority figures. God wants to show you the love of the true Father who loves you with an everlasting and perfect love.

God is not a passive father, but one who pursues His children. He pursued Adam and Eve even as they ran away from Him. The first question God asks in Scripture occurs after Adam and Eve rebelled and hid from God. He walked through the Garden and called out to them, "Where are you?" Although God knew exactly where they were and what they had done, He asked the question for their sake. He wanted Adam and Eve to know He loved them even when they were hiding in guilt and shame because of their sin. Do you remember the horror you felt as a young child when you got separated from your mom or dad in a store, even if only for a few seconds? Do you remember the joy and relief you experienced when you were found? As His child, even in the horror of your sin, you can be assured that the Father still pursues you.

Your Wise and Good Father

Unlike earthly authorities, your heavenly Father is always and only wise and good. God knows everything. However, wisdom is more than just knowing things; it is "know how." Many people have knowledge but fail to apply it well. God's wisdom enables Him to "know how" to do everything perfectly (2 Peter 2:9). In other words, knowledge is like having all the right tools in the toolbox, but wisdom is selecting the right tool to fix what is broken. Being wise also includes having the ability to formulate a plan and carry it out in the best and most effective manner.

God selected Jesus to fix the devastation sin has caused. That's because there is only one solution to the divine dilemma—Jesus. He came to be your solution for sin. He reversed the curse that holds you and all mankind in bondage. The King of Kings put on flesh and was born into poverty and obscurity. He obeyed every one of God's laws, while loving His Father and people perfectly. He sacrificed Himself on the cross to pay the penalty and restore His people to Himself. He was rejected, falsely accused, mocked, beaten, and given a criminal's death on a cross. Jesus willingly took on all the sin and suffering of the world and was separated from the Father in order to reconcile you to the Father (2 Cor. 5:21).

> Stop and consider what it cost Jesus to be your sin solution. Think about the worst pain you have experienced in your life: spiritual, physical, emotional, psychological, relational. Now, add to that every other pain you have endured from your own choices or the choices of others. Now you have the tiniest glimpse of what it meant for Jesus to take the wrath of God for your sin. Write a prayer of thanks to Jesus for enduring the cross for your sake.

God is not only wise; He is also always good. All of the good things you enjoy in life come from Him (James 1:17). Since

God is your Father through your faith in Christ, all of God's attributes work always and only for your good! You might ask how that can be since your life is full of struggles and bad things happen to you. When Adam and Eve were banished from the garden, everything looked disastrous, but God was actually being good to them. He was protecting them from eating from the Tree of Life. Without His goodness, they would have eaten from that tree and sealed their fallen state by living forever in misery.

> Since God is your Father through your faith in Christ, all of God's attributes work only and always for your good!

Many times, what God is doing or what He is asking you to do does not make sense. You cannot see the good. How might reflecting on the cross help you to trust God when you are tempted to question His wisdom?

God is always and only good; yet, often you define "good" according to your own standard. The Psalm writer, Asaph, had to redefine his idea of the goodness of God. He recognized things that were "good" for him were the things that brought him near to God (see Ps. 73:28). Christians often misquote Romans 8:28 to mean that bad things won't happen to them or will end up good in this life: *"And we know that for those who love God all things work together for good, for those who are called according to his purpose."* However, the Scripture goes on to define the good that God is accomplishing, *"For those whom he foreknew he also predestined to be conformed to the image of his Son, in order that he might be the firstborn among many brothers. And those whom he predestined he also called, and those whom he called he also justified, and those whom he justified he also glorified"* (Rom. 8:29–30). The best good that God can do in your life is to give you access to Him through Jesus; this then gives you the power of the Holy Spirit and the privilege of being conformed to the image of Christ who will one day take you home to His eternal kingdom!

Author, A.W. Tozer said, "What comes into our minds when we think about God is the most important thing about us." What three words you would use to describe God?

What you know about God in your head might not be what you actually believe about Him in your heart. How do you know what you REALLY believe? You will know what you really believe by your actions. Are the three words you wrote above reflected in how you act? What would change if you really believed that God is who you say He is?

Daughters of the King

When you trust in Jesus, the Father calls you His daughter and welcomes you into His eternal Kingdom (1 John 3:1). You are adopted forever into a new family with all the rights and privileges of a beloved child. In Christ, you are forgiven of all your sins: past, present, and future. Your record is wiped clean, the penalty for your sin has been paid, and you have the righteousness of Jesus given to you. This means that when God sees you, He sees only the perfect record of Jesus (Philippians 3:9). Not only do you stand forgiven in Christ, but you also have instant and ongoing access to your Father God because of Jesus. You don't have to be afraid to go to Him at any time, in whatever state you might be, and pour out your heart to Him. Since you died with Christ and your life is hidden with Christ in God, you are free to come before His throne with your cries of suffering and confessions of sin (Ps. 62:8; Col. 3:3; 1 John 1:9). Stop running away from Him. He is pursuing you in love. Run to Him. He paid a great price so that you could always run to Him and never have to run away from Him again.

Do you see how much your heavenly Father loves you? It's not because you are lovely, but because He is love and chose to love the unlovable (1 John 4:19). How freeing to know your sins are forgiven and you have access to the Father to confess your sin and find comfort in times of trouble. How do you respond to such a great gift?

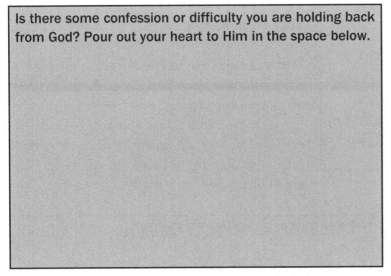

Is there some confession or difficulty you are holding back from God? Pour out your heart to Him in the space below.

Respond to His love for you by loving Him and following Him. Express that love through trust and obedience. Access to the resurrection power of Jesus through the Holy Spirit is your weapon to kill indwelling sin and to bear up under the weight of a sin-cursed world. Although Jesus conquered sin and death at the cross, the fullness of His victory will not be realized until you die, or He returns. In this life, you will continue to wrestle with the sinful desires of your flesh and want to throw in the towel when troubles mount (Gal. 5:19–21; 6:9). Thankfully, your loving Father is committed to using the sin inside you and around you to cultivate humility and dependence on Him. Someone has said, "God loves you just the way you are but too much to let you stay that way." Even if it feels like you will never see the change you want to see, God promises to keep working in you until His work is complete (Phil. 1:6). As you grasp the breadth, length, height and depth of God's love for you in Christ, you will be strengthened in the fight against sin and encouraged to persevere in suffering (Eph. 3:18).

Walk by faith in His power to live out His rule of love. Desires and behaviors will change little by little as you are being transformed into the likeness of Jesus. When you become in practice what you are in position, you will have a new family resemblance: a daughter of the Most High King. And you will want to follow Him because He is sovereign, holy, wise and good. When you live under His loving rule, you are the most free to be all He created you to be and to enjoy all He purchased for you.

> When you become in practice what you are in position, you will have a new family resemblance: a daughter of the Most High King.

Your Coming King

And it gets even better! Jesus is coming back to gather His children to Himself and establish His Kingdom once again here on earth. In this new earth, you will have full access to the King, walking with God like Adam and Eve once did in the Garden. You will finally be free to love Him fully, and nothing will separate you from Him for all of eternity.

"THE KINGDOM LIFE" CHAPTER REVIEW

What doctrinal concepts were new or reinforced for you in this section?

SELF-COUNSEL JOURNAL

Read the Journal Instructions and the Journal Samples for help. (You can also find additional help and blank journal pages at knownministries.org.)

Complete the Self-Counsel Journal to connect your current struggle to how you RELATE to God as Father.

Rule — Relate — Reflect — Represent — Reproduce — Restore — Repeat

RELATE
Self-Counsel Journal Sample
Sample: Diane's Story

Diane admits that viewing God as a loving Father is difficult for her. In this example, you will see her wrestling, and that is good. It is okay to be honest here. We are not looking for right answers, we are looking for honest reflections of your heart so that God's truth can be applied to it.

Relate: God as Father—Am I relating to God as a beloved daughter with all the access and privilege my Father has bestowed on me?

No, and that's hard. The fact that I am such an imperfect parent and my parents were imperfect, it can be difficult to relate to God as a perfectly loving Father. My earthly parenting motivations are so often selfish that it can be a challenge not to have a distorted view of God and his motives toward me.

How does access to God as my Father change the way I handle my sin or suffering?

I know in my mind that I have access to God as my loving Father. I know that I can pray to Him at any time and He will hear me. I know that He already knows my heart completely. I know that He loves me both corporately as a part of Christ's body and individually, as I love my children collectively and individually.

How does reflecting on God's wisdom and goodness at the cross help me in my current struggle?

When I consider the sacrifice that Christ made on my behalf, how can I doubt his love for me, or his goodness? When I consider that God in his wisdom made provision for my sin before the creation of the world, I am overwhelmed.

Am I living as if the penalty of sin has been paid? I am forgiven!

When I realize I am forgiven, I WANT to repent! Lord, please forgive me for wrestling with you for control of my life. Please forgive me for doubting your love for me and that you are a good Father.

Am I living as if the power of sin has been broken? I can obey!

When I rest in Who God is and who He says I am in Him, only then can I stop trying to control my own life and circumstances and stop doubting God's goodness and love for me.

Am I living in light of the fact that the presence of sin will be removed? This will end!

I need to consider my current situation more in light of eternity.

RELATE
Self-Counsel Journal

Chapter 2 Relate: God as Father—***Am I relating to God as a beloved daughter with all the access and privilege my Father has bestowed on me?***

1. How does access to God as my Father change the way I handle my sin or suffering?

2. How does reflecting on God's wisdom and goodness at the cross help me in my current struggle?

3. Am I living as if the penalty of sin has been paid? I am forgiven!

4. Am I living as if the power of sin has been broken? I can obey!

5. Am I living in light of the fact that the presence of sin will be removed? This will end!

Rule Relate Reflect Represent Reproduce Restore Repeat

CHAPTER 3
REFLECT: MADE IN HIS IMAGE

1. Read the chapter and prayerfully answer the questions throughout the study to consider the truth of Reflecting God as an image bearer.

2. Use The Kingdom Life Chapter Review to reflect on the doctrinal truths that are new or reinforced.

3. Use the Self-Counsel Journal page to continue to write about RULE and RELATE. Now add REFLECT to each journal entry. Do as many journal entries as you have need and time. You can copy the journal pages or print more at the website. (See the journal instructions in the Journal Introduction and the sample Self Counsel Journal, Diane's Story, for help. For additional help and examples go to knownministries.org.)

4. If you are meeting with a friend(s), use the Group Discussion Questions in Appendix II.

CHAPTER THREE

REFLECT: MADE IN HIS IMAGE

Scripture: Genesis 1–3

"Then God said, 'Let us make man in our image, after our likeness. And let them have dominion over the fish of the sea and over the birds of the heavens and over the live-stock and over all the earth and over every creeping thing that creeps on the earth.' So God created man in his own image, in the image of God he created him; male and female he created them" (Gen. 1:26-27).

". . . then the LORD God formed the man of dust from the ground and breathed into his nostrils the breath of life, and the man became a living creature" (Gen. 2:7).

Made to Reflect Him

When the King formed the people for His kingdom, He made them completely different from the rest of His creation. The first five days, He spoke all of His creation into existence. But on the sixth day, he crowned His creation with a man and woman made in the image and likeness of the Triune God. He didn't just speak this man and woman into existence. The Bible says that He "breathed into his nostrils the breath of life." In the original language of the Old Testament, the word translated "breathe" can literally refer to breath, but it also can be translated wind, air, or spirit. God didn't just give Adam and Eve air in their lungs; He breathed into them a soul that will live forever. Adam and Eve were made to reflect God's perfect character. They were created in holiness, set apart to please Him and to deal rightly with one another (Eph. 4:24, Col.3:10).

What does it mean to be made in the image of God? It means more than just looking like someone. My daughter looks and sounds like me. When people see her, they may say she is the "spitting image" of me. When you look into a mirror you see a reflection, an image, not the real person. The image reflects something greater. You reflect God. If you want to know what He looks like, in part, you look at humankind. Although each person is stamped with the image of God, you reflect that image individually. Yet God is so gloriously complex that it takes all people, of all times, in all places to reflect just a fraction of His greatness. The last few evenings the most beautiful, yellow harvest moon has shone in the sky. Even in all its beauty, the moon has no light of its own. It is a lesser body that simply reflects the great light of the sun. God stamped you with His likeness in order that you would reflect His great worth to the world (2 Corinthians 3:18).

God stamped you with His likeness in order that you would reflect His great worth to the world (2 Corinthians 3:18).

The Creator King made you in His image. Theologians refer to this as the *imago Dei*, the image of God. God made you to reflect Him in a visible and understandable way to the world. In what ways do you reflect the image of God in current relationships or responsibilities?

God is pleased to share many of His attributes with mankind (love, joy, peace, patience, etc.), but He also reserves for Himself those qualities which make Him God alone (all-knowing, all- seeing, all-controlling, etc.). Even though we do not share all of God's characteristics, we are still able to reflect Him in some small way. For example, when you teach, you reflect the wisdom of God. When you care for your children, you reflect the love of God. When you care for a sick friend, you reflect the mercy of God. While God is the most glorious One, He has shared with you a little bit of His glory.

When you consider this glorious truth, you may be tempted to boast in your glory. However, what makes you special is not you, but the reflection of God in you. This truth should both humble your pride and increase your awe of God. It also causes you to recognize that any view that gives man glory apart from God is incomplete and destructive. One of the most infamous examples in history of stealing God's glory is the Roman emperor, Nero, who declared himself a god and then proceeded to commit all manner of atrocities against Christians and even his own family. All of your praise of man should lead you to a greater praise of God. Just like you don't stand at the edge of the Grand Canyon and declare "Look at me!" Your life should point to the greatness of God!

The image of God stamped on you is what gives you worth. You have no glory of your own; you only have the glory of God reflected in you. As you gaze at the greatness of God, you begin to see the wonder that He would stoop to create you and stamp you with His likeness. King David, who penned many of the Psalms, is perhaps the best-known king in the Old Testament. In Psalm 8, he captures the glory of God and the glory of God in man in a beautiful song of exaltation. Read all of Psalm 8. Using personal pronouns and your own vocabulary, go verse by verse to write your own boast in the Lord.

The image of God stamped on each person means that you have an inherent dignity and worth that cannot be taken away. Your value comes from the image of the King imprinted on you. You may have had the experience of wanting to buy a piece of clothing and being shocked at the price. You can hold two shirts up next to each other that look exactly alike, yet one costs five times the amount of the other. Why is this? The shirt is just a shirt until you stamp it with the logo of the designer. That "stamp" is what gives the one shirt its value. Out of all of God's creation, only man is made in the

> The image of God stamped on each person means that you have an inherent dignity and worth that cannot be taken away.

image of God. You need not look to the world, other people, or your circumstances to tell you what you are worth. Your Creator determines your worth. Pastor Matt Chandler illustrates this with a story comparing his friend, Darrin, who is autistic, to the prize-winning horse, Secretariat:

> "You look at Secretariat, the amount of cash that horse brought in in stud fees because of how he was physiologically built and because of what he accomplished. Darrin, who will never know his ABCs and will never contribute as we have determined contribution should look, is worth far more. It's far more of a tragedy for anything bad to ever happen to Darrin than it would be for anything bad to happen to that horse, not that we want bad things to happen to the horse. Darrin is more valuable and always will be more valuable because Darrin carries within himself the God-like deposit, the imago Dei, made in the image of God."[1]

The three persons of the Godhead existed before the world began, communing, loving, and glorifying one another. Mankind was created to reflect this relational aspect of God. The creation of Adam and Eve is the first and only time in the creation account that God uses the plural, "Us," to refer to Himself. Humans are the only creatures in all of creation who are made out of the overflow of the perfect communion of the three persons of the Godhead. To be made in His image means you are hardwired for relational connection with God and with others. The King pursued relationship with Adam, yet God knew Adam needed other people. He gave Adam a companion, Eve, because God knew Adam needed intimate connections with Himself and with others to be fully human and to be able to fulfill the mission in the kingdom.

Image Distorted

When Adam and Eve sinned, they chose autonomy from the King. As a result, they brutally marred and disfigured the image of God within them (Gen.3:1–19; Rom. 5:12–21). The ability of people to reflect God was distorted. Theologian R.C.

---

1 Matt Chandler, sermon, "In His Image." Accessed February 2019, https://www.tvcresources.net/resource-library/sermons/in-his-image

Sproul refers to this fallen state as "radical corruption." No longer were Adam and Eve set apart just to please God in holiness. No longer were they righteous in their dealings with one another. Sin made all of mankind godless and crooked. Sin taints every part of your being and defiles your mind, body, will, and emotions. Adam and Eve passed down this state of corruption or depravity to you. You are not a sinner because you sin, rather you sin because you are a sinner (Ps. 51:5). The reflection of God in you now looks like the warped reflection in a carnival mirror. You are recognizable, but you are completely distorted and out of proportion. In each human heart lies the capacity for every wickedness and gross sin imaginable. If it were not for the grace of God, you could commit the most vile acts and be counted among the most hated people in human history.

Author and pastor Jack Miller loved to say, "Cheer up! You're a worse sinner than you ever dared imagine, and you're more loved than you ever dared hope." Look up Romans 8:38–39 in The Message, meditate on it, and write it down here in your own words:

One of the most tragic consequences of the fall is the way our view of God has been distorted. You distort the image of God and make Him in your own image when you believe He is not powerful enough, not wise enough, or not good enough. Because of sin, the apostle Paul says your current understanding of God is like looking through a dim mirror (1 Cor. 13:12). Ancient mirrors were usually crafted of metal which gave a reflection of a person's face that was barely recognizable. Your knowledge of God is often based on that kind of distortion and incomplete knowledge. As a consequence, you don't accurately reflect the truth of the glory of God. However, as you grow in your knowledge of God by seeing Him more clearly in His word and as you live to obey Him, your life more closely reflects who He is and brings Him glory.

Image Renewed

In order to repair the image of God in you, God sent His Son, Jesus, to die for your sins. You were made in the image of God, but Jesus *is* the image of God, the **Imago Dei** (Col. 1:15). On the cross, Jesus, the perfect Image of God, had to be destroyed in order to renew the image of God in you (Rom. 8:28–30). Jesus perfectly lived holiness and righteousness in order to become the perfect sacrifice to pay the penalty for your sin. He also became your holiness and righteousness so that you can stand before God with a perfect record (1 Cor. 1:30, Luke 1:74-75). When you trust in Jesus, you are declared holy and righteous, but God continues to transform your conduct to be holy and righteous in practice. He recreates you in the image of Christ in order to regain what was lost in the fall. The Bible calls this ongoing process of image renewal sanctification (Phil. 1:6). In sanctification, the Holy Spirit changes you to believe what God says and to practice that in obedience. The more you become like Jesus, the more "human" you really are, because you are becoming what you were created to be. C.S. Lewis said, "Each day we are either becoming a creature of splendid glory or one of unthinkable horror." The more a person looks like Jesus (loving God and neighbor) the more human they become but the less they look like Jesus (hating God and neighbor) the less human they become.

William Golding clearly depicted this dehumanization in his novel, *Lord of the Flies*. Stranded on an island, proper British boys turned to savages when left to rule themselves. You may see this tendency in yourself. Road rage is a common example of how a calm and rational person can be changed into a screaming maniac in just a few short moments. Another example may occur in your relationships; have you ever dehumanized yourself and another person by the way that you talked to or about them? Think of a time when you acted under your own rule and woke up to the knowledge that you were being less than human?

The Holy Spirit is remaking you as a Christian to be like Jesus (Col. 1:15). The process is often slow because, in your flesh, you resist change. However, God is committed to renewing your heart and conduct in order to restore elements of the image of God in you that were lost or damaged in the Fall. Author Paul Tripp says, "In grace, He leads you where you didn't plan to go in order to produce in you what you could not achieve on your own. He works to order the values of your heart so that you let go of your little kingdom of one and give yourself to His Kingdom of glory and grace."

The Holy Spirit uses His two main tools: the Word of God and the people of God. The Spirit uses the Word to teach, rebuke, correct and train you (2 Tim. 3:16-17). In addition, there are some things you learn about God and yourself only when you are in meaningful relationships with other believers. Paul prays that you know the great love of God for you. He says you will comprehend it "with all the saints" (Eph. 3:17–19). Your understanding of God is incomplete without fellowship with others, and so is your understanding of yourself. You cannot see your own heart clearly; you need the Word of God and the people of God to help you to recognize your blind spots and gently point them out (Heb. 3:13).

> **As you represent the Triune community, are you intentionally investing in the lives of others in ways that are meaningful for them and for yourself?**
>
> **As you long to reflect His glory, do you allow others the freedom to speak truth to you when you get off track?**

God takes great pleasure in you, but He also created you to take pleasure in Him. When you take pleasure in Him, you bring Him glory. The word glory in the Bible means weight. As you grow in your pleasure of Him, your desire for Him should outweigh any other desire in your heart, including your desire for self-rule. When you live to make Him famous, to give Him glory, your life becomes an act of worship to the King. Author Ed Welch says it this way:

> "In the kingdom of God, our eyes are turned away from ourselves and onto the glory of the King. In this simple redirection we have the pleasure of thinking of ourselves less. If Jesus is highly honored because He gives us such a great gift, then we bring it on. I'll gladly accept it. I love this whole idea that living for His glory frees me from the tyranny of myself!"[2]

The Final Chapter: Full Restoration

One glorious day, we will be who God created us to be. The image of God will be fully restored in us. All the effects of the fall will be reversed. We will realize the full weight of His glory when He returns to claim His people and set up His rule of love in the New Heavens and the New Earth. We will see Jesus, without distortion or error, as He truly is in all of His perfection and glory. Only then will we perfectly reflect Him in the righteousness and holiness as we were created to do (Luke 1:24-25; 1 John 3:2).

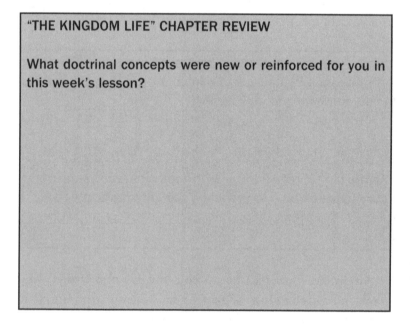

"THE KINGDOM LIFE" CHAPTER REVIEW

What doctrinal concepts were new or reinforced for you in this week's lesson?

---

2 Ed Welch, *Shame Interrupted: How God Lifts the Pain of Worthlessness and Rejection.* New Growth Press, 2012.

Read the Journal Instructions and the Journal Samples for help. (You can also find additional help and blank journal pages at knownministries.org.)

Complete the Self-Counsel Journal to connect your current struggle to how you REFLECT God as an image-bearer.

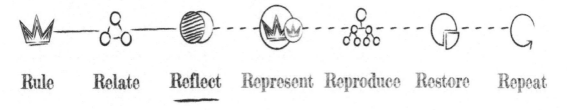

Rule   Relate   **Reflect**   Represent   Reproduce   Restore   Repeat

REFLECT
Self-Counsel Journal Sample
Sample: Diane's Story

As Diane struggles with her family's relocation, she begins to recognize the lies she believes about God and how she can replace those lies with the truth of who He really is. This recognition will help her to respond in a way that shows Christ to her family.

Reflect: Made in His Image—Am I glorifying God by reflecting Him as a redeemed image bearer?

In what ways am I striving to be God, instead of being like God?

Instead of trusting God who sees the whole picture, eternity past to eternity future, I think that I know what is best for me and my family. I wrongly think that I see my circumstances rightly.

Am I placing value on what God says is valuable or am I allowing someone or something else to define worth?

Instead of trusting that God loves me and has a beautiful and perfect plan for me and my family, I am choosing to value my comfort and my security and putting my comfort and security in things that don't deliver. My house and community do not and cannot provide real comfort and security—only Christ can.

Have I rightly understood the depth of my sinfulness due to image distortion?

My thinking is so selfish. I acknowledge that my husband is happy in his new job, yet I place my own desires above his. And worse, I acknowledge that I KNOW that it is God's will and provision for us to move. He has given me such peace and assurance of that, yet my sinful, selfish heart still chooses to hold tight to my own desires. In this struggle, I am not loving God and others more than myself.

In what ways have I made God in my image, believing lies and distortions about Him?

I've believed that same lie that Eve believed—that God is holding out on me. In very subtle ways, I tell myself that if God really cared about me, he would give me what I want. While my head knows that He loves me and that His ways are higher than my ways, my sinful heart lies.

How can I reflect God's worth, weight, and renown as I struggle with my sin/suffering?

I can choose to take those thoughts captive to what I know to be true. I can choose to reflect on who God is and remember His character and attributes.

How can I depend on the Holy Spirit, God's Word, and other Christians for the truth?

I have to fight my tendency to "retreat to my cave" and insulate myself from the truth. I have to pray, asking the Lord to reveal my heart and confess what He shows me. I have to rest in the knowledge that the Word of God is the only message that is trustworthy. My heart will lie to me all day long, but the Word of God is always the plumb line. I have to stay engaged in relationships with other believers and ask them to hold me accountable to the Truth over my fears and emotions.

How am I rejoicing in the good God is producing in my circumstance (Christ-likeness) knowing this is His ultimate goal for me?

I can't see the good right now, but I know that He is using this to conform me to His image because His Word promises that He uses everything and nothing is wasted.

Rule: God as King—*Am I living under the absolute rule of the Most High King of the Universe in my heart and life?*

Relate: God as Father—*Am I relating to God as a beloved daughter with all the access and privilege my Father has bestowed on me?*

Reflect: Made in His Image—*Am I glorifying God by reflecting Him as a redeemed image bearer?*

1. In what ways am I striving to **be** God, instead of being **like** God?

2. Am I placing value on what God says is valuable, or am I allowing someone or something else to define worth?

3. Have I rightly understood the depth of my sinfulness due to image distortion?

4. In what ways have I made God in my image believing lies and distortions about Him?

5. How can I reflect God's worth, significance and renown as I struggle with my sin/suffering?

6. How can I depend on the Holy Spirit, God's Word, and other Christians for_____?

7. How am I rejoicing in the good God is producing in my circumstance (Christ-likeness) knowing this is His ultimate goal for me?

Rule   Relate   Reflect   Represent   Reproduce   Restore   Repeat

CHAPTER 4
REPRESENT: MADE BY HIS DESIGN

1. Read the chapter and prayerfully answer the questions throughout the study to consider the truth of representing God as a helper.

2. Use The Kingdom Life Chapter Review to reflect on the doctrinal truths that are new or reinforced.

3. Use the Self-Counsel Journal page to continue to write about RULE, RELATE, and REFLECT. Now add REPRESENT to each journal entry. Do as many journal entries as you have need and time. You can copy the journal pages or print more at the website. (See the journal instructions in the Journal Introduction and the sample Self Counsel Journal, Diane's Story, for help. For additional help and examples go to known-ministries.org.)

4. If you are meeting with a friend(s), use the Group Discussion Questions in Appendix II.

CHAPTER FOUR

REPRESENT: MADE BY HIS DESIGN

Scripture: Genesis 1
"So God created man in his own image, in the image of God he created him; male and female he created them."
Genesis 1:27

God as our Designer

Our Creator dictates our design. When you hear the word design, what comes to mind? You may think of decorating a house, building a website, or creating the latest fashions. If you have ever built a house, you know the importance of design both inside and outside the house. Design gives purpose and beauty to every aspect of creating a home, and it begins when an architect draws up the structure for the house. These design plans become blueprints. As the construction takes shape, the process of design moves inside the house, as the decorator begins to choose the pretties: paint colors, light fixtures, appliances and finishing touches. Throughout each step of the process, the design guides those working on the house to bring about the beautiful and functional home the owner envisions.

You Are His Ambassador

God is our designer. He created everything for His own glory. He made both man and woman in His glorious image to represent Him on earth as an ambassador. An ambassador is a person who acts in the name of another. As God's ambassador, you were created to demonstrate and maintain His loving rule over the world. The apostle Paul told the church at Corinth, ***"Therefore, we are ambassadors for Christ, God making his appeal through us. We implore you on behalf of Christ, be reconciled to God"*** (2 Cor. 5:20). You may be wondering how you could possibly speak on the King's behalf. In order to do so, you must know Him well as He has revealed Himself in His Word, and you must operate with the power of His Spirit living within you. God has authorized you as His emissary to act and speak on His behalf in order that His plan for humanity's reconciliation to Him would spread to all the earth.

Helper Design

When the King made Adam and Eve, He did not make them identical. He fashioned them "male and female." Even the materials used to make the man and woman were different. Adam was spoken into being and made from the dust of the ground, but Eve was taken from the flesh of the man. You don't have to look to the biblical account to see that men and women are different. You just have to look at men and women.

> Knowing that God is both your ruling king and your loving Father means that you can trust that His design for you is both right and good.

Knowing that God is both your ruling king and your loving Father means that you can trust that His design for you is both right and good. God fashioned you as a woman to be an *ezer.* *Ezer,* of course, is the Hebrew word translated "helper" in Genesis 2:18. Ever since the fall and the ensuing curse (Gen. 2:16), people have attempted to deconstruct God's good and unique helper design resulting in distortions of the truth and the oppression of women. Unfortunately, our culture understands the word "helper" as one who is weak and inferior. You may even consider a helper role as someone who is functioning as a subordinate, in a "less than" capacity compared to the real "movers and shakers." It might be helpful to think of it this way: is the doctor less than the patient? Is the mother less than the child? Is the teacher less than her student? In each example, you would not say the helper is inferior. You would simply argue for the importance and necessity of the helper. So, it was with the first woman. Adam needed help before the fall. Husbands have needed help ever since. Your helper-design tendency is actually a commentary on men. They need help! Adam could not fulfill the mission God gave him apart from Eve. He needed her in order to be fruitful and multiply and to subdue, tend, and keep God's earth. Only after God created Eve did He step back and call creation, "very good" (Gen. 1:31). Even after the fall, God elevated women's helper design once again when He chose to use a woman to bring forth the Savior of the world. God used the womb, the breasts, and the nurturing hands of a woman to help the Savior grow and become the man who would pay the penalty of sin for the whole world and reconcile humanity to God.

God's helper design does not devalue women to be "less than" their male counterparts. However, it also does not esteem women to be "just like" or even "better than" men. All people, male and female, are made in the image of God and therefore have inherent dignity and worth (Gen. 1:27). However, God did make women distinct and not "just like" men. Your helper design is the particular way you live as an image bearer. You are not "less than," "just like," or "better than."

> God designed you as a helper, equal in essence with man, yet different in the way you live out your purpose.

God designed you as a helper, equal in essence with man, yet different in the way you live out your purpose.

How have you lived out of a "less than" design for women?

How have you lived out of a "just like" design for women?

How have you lived out of a "better than" design for women

God as Helper

In the Old Testament the Hebrew word for helper, *ezer,* is most often used as a reference to God. It comes from a root word that expresses power and strength and speaks of someone who protects, aids, supports, advocates, and surrounds. *Strong's Concordance* defines it as "absolute help." *Ezer* is used twenty-one times in the Old Testament. Sixteen of those are used in a military context to describe God as a powerful helper who saves His people in times of trouble. As an *ezer,* you are a warrior designed to work alongside men to carry out the mission of God's kingdom. Since the first couple lived in the Garden, God's people have been engaged in warfare against the world, the flesh, and the devil. More than ever, God's warrior-women need to understand and embrace His glorious and strong helper design since the culture seeks to undermine the King and His kingdom.

The Other "Helpers" of the Godhead

God is not the only helper seen in Scripture. As the story of the kingdom of God unfolds, you see each member of the Trinity model what a true helper looks like. Each member of the Godhead is co-equal and co-eternal but has different roles within the Godhead. Where would you be without each member of the Trinity helping you both temporally and eternally? You desperately need help from the Father, Son, and Holy Spirit to be the helper God wants you to be!

In the New Testament, God reveals Jesus as the Ultimate Helper. Jesus willingly became a weaker vessel by coming to earth as a man. He became the Ultimate Helper when He did what no man could do, live a sinless life and then die in order to save His children from sin and death. You become a helper like Jesus when you choose to lay down your life in sacrificial love to those He places around you.

> As a woman of God, you <u>are</u> a helper, and you <u>have</u> a Helper.

This task sounds overwhelming and impossible. That's why you still need a Helper today. When Jesus rose from the dead and ascended back to heaven, He left help for believers in the form of the Holy Spirit, who is called the "Helper." First, He helps you by giving you the gift of faith to know God and His love for you. Then, the Holy Spirit comes to live inside you. He helps you remember and utilize the truth of Scripture as you engage in your daily warfare against the world, the flesh, and the devil. He helps you to overcome sin by convicting you and giving you the power to resist temptation. And He helps you by comforting you in the midst of the struggle and by giving you understanding of what you read in God's Word. As a woman of God, you *are* a helper, and you *have* a Helper. The Holy Spirit empowers you to live on the mission God has given you! The world may have an inferior view of the helper design, but God's view of helper is strong, essential, and multi-faceted.

Now that you see the fullness of the word "helper," how does it change your view of being made as a helper?

Helper as an Essential Ally

You can see when God talks about "helper," He is not describing ordinary help. God has even more to say about your design as helper. He said that you are to be a "helper fit" for man (Gen 2:18). This word, "fit," is the Hebrew word **kenegdo**. It occurs only once in Scripture, and it means "corresponding; equal and adequate to himself." One beautiful way you can see corresponding parts is in Olympic pairs figure skating. Each skater is strong and graceful, yet if they try to dominate and compete with each other they will never be able to win.

The idea of "helper fit" also means essential or indispensable. You can see this idea on display right in front of you: your two hands. Your right hand and left hand are mirror images of each other. They are the same, yet different. Each hand has its own unique function, yet you need those two corresponding parts. Have you ever tried to button your jeans, open a jar of spaghetti sauce, or tie a shoe with only one hand? Some functions cannot be done without both of your hands. God made women essential to humanity in families, churches, and communities. The world cannot do without your help!

When you put these two terms together you can see the fullness of your God-given design. You are an **ezer-kenegdo**, a helper fit—a necessary, corresponding helper. Another way to say this is that you are an essential ally ready to help—give aid, balm, remedy, cooperation, and support to those around you.

As a woman you play many roles. For instance, you may be a wife, mother, daughter, sister, co-worker, neighbor, and friend. However, your roles are not the same as your helper design. You may often hear the design of woman discussed primarily as the role of a wife. Interestingly, God forged Eve's design before Adam and Eve were united in marriage. Every woman is born a helper no matter what roles she plays. You are a helper whether you are single or married. You are a helper whether you are the boss or an employee. You are a helper whether you are an accountant or a nurse. What does this mean for single women? If you are single, Jesus is your husband, and you are called to help Him in unique ways. The apostle Paul makes it clear that a single person can have an undivided devotion to the Lord (1 Cor. 7:32–35).

Regardless of your role you were made to help. Whom are you helping? You either help God and His kingdom, or you help an opposing kingdom. God's transforming grace compels the Christian woman to help *for* Him. You are designed as a powerful helper and compelled by grace in order to advance the kingdom of God.

- You advance God's kingdom when you speak truth and encouragement to your husband versus nagging him or complaining against Him.

- You advance God's kingdom when you devote time to the Word, prayer, and fellowship versus allowing other things to take priority.

- You advance God's kingdom when you overcome evil with good in the workplace versus retaliating against your coworker.

> **Make a list of some of the roles that you play. Have you ever considered the difference between your role and your design? What difference would it make to view yourself first as a helper/warrior?**

Regardless of your role, you were made by God's design for His mission. You bring your own distinct femininity to the ministry and mission of God! With God you have the greatest freedom to operate within your helper design for His glory. This means that all women are not cut from the same cookie cutter. Cultural norms should not dictate femininity. For some, femininity means sports, math (and science), and pants! For others, femininity means tea parties, poetry, and dresses. There is room in God's kingdom for different expressions of femininity as long as the helper design is not lost. We express that helper design through gifts and abilities in thousands of ways.

> Oftentimes in your various roles, your helper design enables you to see what is missing so that you can help to fill in those gaps.

So, go be helpers using your God-given design in your various roles to advance the kingdom of God.

The Bible gives guidelines for how a woman's design is uniquely expressed in two very specific roles: her function in marriage and in the local church. (However, there are very godly women who may see this differently.) These roles in marriage and in the church are not "lesser than" designations. In fact, women are essential allies in both the home and the church. While many in these God-ordained institutions often fail to recognize the significance of the helper design, the flaw is in human execution, not in God's design.

God has designed you as a woman to be a helper, an essential ally to recognize deficits. Oftentimes in your various roles, your helper design enables you to see what is missing so that you can help to fill in those gaps. Whether this ability to see shortcomings is a blessing or a burden depends on your response. If you choose to see only shortcomings and become critical, you will often resort to complaining or comparing. These responses deny the purpose of your design, undermine those around you, and steal glory from God. When you find yourself tempted to be a critic, recognize that God is showing you those deficits and consider how He may be calling you to be an essential ally. Here are a few examples:

- One church member recognized that the widows in her church were being overlooked. Instead of blaming the leadership, she organized some women to call these widows to inquire about their needs and to invite them to events.

- A young, single woman took a job in a family-owned business where everyone was overworked and exhausted. She quietly worked hard to learn as much of the business as she could and to have a great attitude at work every day. When she left for the mission field they couldn't believe how much they had come to rely on her in one short year.

- A close friend realized that her neighbor was struggling with grief and isolation. She listened to her neighbor for a time and then connected her to a counselor and with a women's Bible study where she could have support and fellowship.

> Think of one area where you find yourself being critical. Write out two practical ways that you can become an essential ally to help in that situation.

A World Without Helpers

Storyteller Sean Dietrich wrote a blog called "Sugar and Spice" in which he sums up the essence of womanhood and helping in a beautiful way. During the week following his father's funeral, women who loved him descended on his home—cooking, cleaning, and caring. He remembers:

The week after Daddy's funeral, it stormed. Bad. I woke to the sound of wind. Rain.

And piano music.

I walked downstairs to see our den full of ladies dusting, sweeping, mopping. One woman was even playing our hallway spinet.

"Morning," said my aunt, kissing my forehead. "You want breakfast?"

No. I didn't.

I hadn't been hungry for weeks. I'd lost weight because of it. The only things I could choke down were milkshakes. And it's because of this, I haven't touched one since my voice dropped.

My aunt led me to the kitchen.

It was crowded. Ladies in aprons, standing at workstations, dusting things with flour. Almost every surface held poundcakes, layer cakes, bundt cakes, or cookies.

I received three hugs, ten kisses, and one stiff pat on the hindsection.

My aunt made a milkshake by hand, then said, "Get some chocolate cake, too. It's GOT to get eaten before it goes bad."

That woman. She was made of sugar and spice, and all kinds of bacon grease.

I wandered to the porch, sipping a milkshake, eating cake. I found my uncle on the swing, listening to the rain make noise, the same sound TV static makes.

"Ain't they something?" he said, spitting into a mug. "All them busy ladies."

"Yeah."

He laughed. "You know what they call life without women?"

"What?"

"They call it suffering."

Well, I'd counted nearly twelve females in our house—not including the piano-player. Laughter came from the kitchen. Music from the den. I guess we weren't suffering too bad.

Then, the screen door slapped. A young lady came onto the porch with two more plates of chocolate cake.

My uncle stood when he saw the girl. I stood with him—which is something my people do in the presence of females.

He thank-you-ma'amed her. So did I.

He handed me his cake and said, "You're gonna have to eat mine, I already gotta mouthful of spit."

So, I did.

Anyway, yesterday I woke to the sounds of thunder. A pine tree behind our house got hit by lightning. The apocalyptic noise rattled me awake.

And when I wandered out of the bedroom, I expected to see our house torn apart.

I didn't. What I found was our kitchen, humming with energy. And it took me back in time. My wife had prepared breakfast big enough for a first-string varsity lineup.

She said, "I sure as hell hope you're hungry."

Hungry. As it happens, nowadays I am hungry—though sometimes this world tries to steal a man's appetite. And I'm more than that. I'm alive.

And none of it was my doing. It was God's own army who saved me. Wingless ambassadors, who've taken the time to water me like a house-plant.

They may look like aunts, mamas, sisters, and wives. But they're far more than that.

They are women.

And life without them is called suffering.[3]

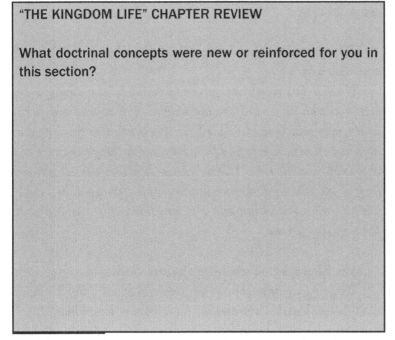

Name one or two women in your life that if they were taken away your life would surely suffer. In what ways would you suffer? In what ways would life without YOU be called suffering?

Helpers in the Coming Kingdom

When Jesus comes again to bring His kingdom in the new heavens and earth, all of His children will reign with Him and serve with Him for all eternity. It is hard to imagine what life will be like without the battle of the sexes, isn't it? That shows you how deeply ingrained the animosity between the sexes has become. However, one day, you will be fully restored as an image bearer in your helper design as you work alongside men without comparison or competition as a helper for your eternal King (Rev. 22:5).

"THE KINGDOM LIFE" CHAPTER REVIEW

What doctrinal concepts were new or reinforced for you in this section?

3 Sean Dietrich, "Sugar and Spice," used by permission from the author, from www. seandietrich.com

Read the Journal Instructions and the Journal Samples for help. (You can also find additional help and blank journal pages at knownministries.org.)

Complete the Self-Counsel Journal to connect your current struggle to how you REPRESENT God as a helper.

Rule   **Relate**   **Reflect**   **Represent**   **Reproduce**   **Restore**   **Repeat**

REPRESENT
Self-Counsel Journal Sample
Diane's Story

We know that as Diane's family moves, she will have the opportunity to be a helper in many physical ways, but through the journal questions she will explore how she can help her family spiritually as they make this transition.

Represent: Made by His Design—Am I helping God as essential ally?

Where am I being tempted to abandon my job as an essential ally?

When I fail to encourage my husband by wallowing in my own fear and anxiety, I am not helping him to lead our family in the way that God has called us. When I fail to encourage my daughter in her anxiety and fear, I am not helping her in the way that God has called me. When I choose to wallow in self-pity over leaving my church and other ministry opportunities that I love, I am not helping God to build His kingdom in the places that He has prepared for me.

Am I helping or working against God?

When I give in to my anxiety and selfishness, I am hindering God. When I walk in the truth, I am helping for Him.

What deficits do I see? How am I being critical or complaining? How would help come through me?

I can justify that I'm not being critical because my words are generally not critical or complaining, but my thoughts and attitudes often are critical and complaining and that probably spills over to my words and tone more often than I'm even aware.

Am I comparing myself to others? How is this hurting my ability to help?

Am I creating suffering or alleviating suffering? What needs to change for others to say, "Life without her is suffering."

While wanting to believe that moving will create suffering for my daughter, deep in my heart I know that's not true. It may be hard on her and on me, but God's character can be trusted to use the hard things to conform us to His image. He will be with us and He will strengthen us. He will use all of it for our good and His glory. If I could walk in that, I would alleviate my self-inflicted suffering. Instead, I often create suffering by projecting my own anxiety onto my other family members.

REPRESENT
Self-Counsel Journal

Rule: God as King—*Am I living under the absolute rule of the Most High King of the Universe in my heart and life?*

Relate: God as Father—*Am I relating to God as a beloved daughter, with all the access and privilege my Father has bestowed on me?*

Reflect: Made in His Image—*Am I glorifying God by reflecting Him as a redeemed image bearer?*

Represent: Made by His Design—*Am I helping God as His essential ally?*

1. Where am I being tempted to abandon my job as an essential ally?

2. Am I helping or working against God?

3. What deficits do I see? How am I being critical or complaining? How would help come through me?

4. Am I comparing myself to others? How is this hurting my ability to help?

5. Am I creating suffering or alleviating suffering? What needs to change for others to say, "Life without her is suffering."

NOTES

CHAPTER 5
REPRODUCE: MADE TO MULTIPLY

1. Read the chapter and prayerfully answer the questions throughout the study t consider the truth of Reproducing in the Kingdom.

2. Use The Kingdom Life Chapter Review to reflect on the doctrinal truths that are new or reinforced.

3. Use the Self-Counsel Journal page to continue to write about RULE, RELATE, REFLECT, and REPRESENT. Now add REPRODUCE to each journal entry. Do as many journal entries as you have need and time. You can copy the journal pages or print more at the website. (See the journal instructions in the Journal Introduction and the sample Self Counsel Journal, Diane's Story, for help. For additional help and examples, go to knownministries.org.)

4. If you are meeting with a friend(s), use the Group Discussion Questions in Appendix II.

Rule   Relate   Reflect   Represent   Reproduce   Restore   Repeat

REPRODUCE: MADE TO MULTIPLY

Scripture: Genesis 1

"And God blessed them. And God said to them, 'Be fruitful and multiply and fill the earth....'" **Genesis 1:28**

Kings make edicts. These pronouncements are carried throughout their kingdom and repeated so all the people of the land know the king's law. Important matters warrant repeating. In Genesis 1:22-28, in the span of six verses, the King of the Universe makes a decree and then repeats it. These instructions must be significant! God told Adam and Eve, *"Be fruitful and multiply and fill the earth"* (Gen. 1:28). Of all the conversations God could have had with them in the garden, this instruction is recorded twice! What exactly is God saying to Adam and Eve here? He is commissioning them to fill the earth with worshipers who would show His worth by following Him. To worship something is to give adoration and devotion to it. As an image bearer you were made to worship. You will either worship God, the Creator of all things, or the things that He has created (Rom. 1:18–23).

Fast forward from the Garden of Eden to New Testament times, as Jesus leaves earth to return to heaven. He explicitly commands His disciples to expand His kingdom by reproducing themselves spiritually. Christians call this decree "The Great Commission," and some theologians say it is a restatement of the command God gave to Adam and Eve to *"Be fruitful and multiply."* Christ's final words declare His absolute rule for all time and the greatest privilege and responsibility of every believer, ***"All authority in heaven and on earth has been given to me. Go therefore and make disciples of all nations, baptizing them in the name of the Father and of the Son and of the Holy Spirit, teaching them to observe all that I have commanded you. And behold, I am with you always, to the end of the age,"*** (Matthew 28:18–20). Jesus expands on the command to multiply by giving it a spiritual dimension. He instructs His disciples to multiply worshipers by telling others about His kingship and showing them how to live life in His kingdom.

Imitating King Jesus

Jesus is the original disciplemaker. He called each one of His disciples to, ***"Come follow me . . ."*** (Matt. 4:19). A disciple is a person who follows a leader in order to learn from that person, emulate the leader's life, and pass on lessons learned to others. You become a Christian disciple when you respond to the call of Jesus in faith and pledge your allegiance and loyalty to Him (1 John 2:3). Imitation is at the heart of discipleship. Once you respond to the call, you pattern your life after your Master (1 John 2:6). This manner of life is the way that you worship Him. You may think that worship is what you do at church, but really all of life is worship when it is lived as an act of faith in Christ. As you care for your children, show diligence in school, or have integrity in your business dealings, you are worshiping God with your life. The first believers were called Christians because they had a striking resemblance to their leader, Jesus (Acts 11:26). Just like these early believers, the more you worship Him the more you will resemble Christ in character and in deeds

The first step in becoming a disciple maker is to be a worshiper of the king yourself. Your motivation to evangelism and discipleship comes as you understand that God is the only one who is worthy of worship and that the greatest good you could do for your neighbors is to help them move to a right relationship with Him. Worship captures your affections for Christ and leads you

> The first step in becoming a disciple maker is to be a worshiper of the king yourself.

to put His love into action in your life. The Holy Spirit helps you display God's glory by valuing God and His ways more than anything else in your life. You show your knowledge of Christ's value through faithful obedience to Him. You show that you value Christ more than the approval of others when you choose to speak up when someone uses a racial slur. You show that you value Christ more than your own comfort when you serve others without complaining.

This does not mean that you will perfectly worship God as King. Because God created you a worshiper, you will find your heart worshiping (treasuring, valuing, placing your hope in) many things throughout the course of any given day. Sometimes those desires are sinful (coveting a friend's children or job). Oftentimes, the desires that capture the heart are not sinful, but you place them above your desire for the King. A life of worship to the King means your life will be characterized by turning away from false gods and turning back to Him in faith.

Your life of worship will draw others to Him (evangelism) and teach others to follow Him (discipleship). Look at the illustration below. Each person you encounter is represented somewhere on this wheel from "dead in sin" to mature worshiper of Christ. Every encounter you have with another person is an opportunity to locate where they are on this transformation wheel and to help them move forward to maturity in Christ.

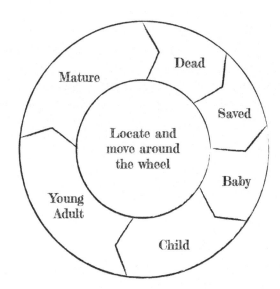

Based on what you have read so far, what views on spiritual reproduction have encouraged and challenged you? How are these views revealed in your passion for Christ, in evangelism, or in your discipleship of others? How do you currently see spiritual reproduction playing out in your life?

Proclaiming King Jesus to Non-Christians

Evangelism is proclaiming the good news that God is king, through your life and words, to those who are not under His rule. Typically, the best opportunities to point non-Christians to Christ arise in the context of authentic relationships. This means you must be developing and maintaining connections with non-Christians. If you survey the Bible, you will find Jesus consistently making friends with His neighbors, His enemies, the outcast, and the most vile of sinners. If you are going to advance the kingdom of King Jesus, you too must offer friendship to those outside the household of faith in hopes of leading them to the Savior.

Look at your circle of relationships. What non-Christians are you intentionally seeking to build relationships with? If you don't have anyone, take a few minutes to think about who you naturally see or spend time with. You don't have to go out of your way to approach people. Just think about those whom God has already put in your path. Write down one or two people God brings to mind whom you could commit to pray for and be more intentional in building a relationship.

Proclaiming through Life

In the context of your relationships, your life becomes the first and most obvious witness to the good news of Christ's kingdom. Witness is often the precursor to evangelism! Your witness is both your life and your words. Jesus laid down His life for sinners by putting aside His rights and privileges in order to advance God's kingdom (Phil. 2:1–11). Like Jesus, you have many opportunities to serve others. When you serve as others as Christ serves His kingdom, you display biblical love and exhibit spiritual fruit: love, joy, peace, patience, kindness,. (1 Cor. 13: 4–8, Gal. 5:22–23). As you walk by faith, living under God's rule in personal holiness and right relationships, you put the life of Christ on display without ever saying a word. (John 3:21, Phil. 2:3–4).

Proclaiming through Listening

Women long for relationships where they are known, understood, and accepted. As you seek to reach other women as new followers of Christ, you will gain access to speak by listening first and listening well. This means listening to know the person, not listening just to "truth" them (zinging them with a Bible verse without any care or time invested). No one likes an intruder. If you sit with people long enough and they know you care for them deeply, they will often invite you to speak into their lives. Again, there is no need to be in a rush. God is not in a rush. You are a constant witness through simply living your life of worshiping Christ until He gives you the opportunity to speak of the One you treasure.

> **Using the one or two people you listed above, write out:**
>
> 1. **How can you practically incarnate Christ to them?**
>
> 2. **How can you learn her story and gain entrance into her life by listening?**

Proclaiming through Telling

God has given you the best way to share His truth through a very familiar story—your story! The most powerful "tool" you have to share the Good News is by telling others what Jesus has done and is doing for you. The Bible gives many examples of evangelism done through personal story. The woman at the well encounters Jesus and then tells her story to the whole town (John 4). The man who is possessed by demons longs to travel with Jesus, but Jesus sends him back to tell his village how he had been healed (Mark 5:18–20). The Apostle Paul had an encounter with Jesus on the road to Damascus then spends the rest of his life telling others how he had been changed (Acts 9:1–19).

> Your story puts His saving and transforming power on display in a powerful way.

Your story puts His saving and transforming power on display in a powerful way. One often overlooked doorway to sharing the gospel happens through your own personal failures and suffering. Most likely, your best platform to "preach" is an area of hurt or struggle. Don't be afraid to reveal how weak, frail, and broken you really are in front of unbelieving family and friends. Your faith in Jesus during times of struggle is a wonderful way to reveal your trust in the King who is your Father. And when you recognize and repent of failure, you demonstrate your faith in your Father who is the King. What weakness could you share to show your trust in the King who is your Father?

Think through your own story using the R's presented thus far in this study:

RULE: How did you live in God's kingdom without any true knowledge of the King? What was your religious background? What/who were you worshiping/living for?

RELATE: When did you come to recognize that your Father made a way for you to come back to Him through Christ? What events drove you to Christ? Who or what did God use to share the good news with you?

> **REFLECT:** What transformation has taken place in your life since you trusted Christ? How do you see Him restoring the image of God in you as He makes you more like Jesus? How have you failed to reflect Christ's image to others, and what do you do when you fail? How have you endured the effects of the fall of mankind into sin, and how has Christ helped you with this?
>
> **REPRESENT:** Where has Christ placed you to represent Him as an ambassador, and how are you doing that?
>
> Now that you have written out your personal testimony share your story with three people this week. Part of being prepared "in season and out of season to give a reason for the hope within you" (2 Tim. 4:2) is practice! You can share your story with unbelievers or share it to encourage fellow believers in the faith (Heb.10:24).

Proclaiming through Sharing the Good News

At some point when God gives you an opportunity, you want to be prepared to lead a person to faith in Jesus. Jesus did not come to simply live a good life or to do good works. He came with a message to save men, women, boys, and girls from the penalty, power, and presence of sin. He preached, ***"Repent of your sins and turn to God, for the Kingdom of Heaven is near"*** (Matt. 4:17). This is the message we must be ready to proclaim as well. Pastor John MacArthur says, "Souls are won to Christ by those prepared to win souls when God chooses to use them." It does not have to be complicated. Through an easily remembered "ABC method," you can compel others to the following actions:

ADMIT to God that you are a sinner.

BELIEVE in Jesus Christ as God's Son who paid the penalty for you.

CONFESS your faith in Jesus Christ as Savior and Lord.

You are called to be faithful to live and proclaim the glory of the King, but God alone is the giver of faith that is needed to repent and believe (Eph. 2:8-9). The apostle Paul told the Corinthians that believers are the aroma of Christ to God. Second Corinthians 2:15-17 (NLT) says, ***"To those who are perishing, we are a dreadful smell of death and doom. But to those who are being saved, we are a life-giving perfume. And who is adequate for such a task as this?"*** Remember that to some people the gospel stinks, so you will stink! However, to those God is drawing near the gospel message is a good fragrance, and you will smell sweet to them as well!

Proclaiming King Jesus to Christians

Reproducing is not just telling non-Christians about Jesus (evangelism); it is also helping believers apply His rule to all of life (discipleship). Jesus' final decree included, "*. . . **teaching them to observe all that I have commanded you**"* (Matt. 28:18-20, bold text added for emphasis). The word "teaching" in the Greek means to "cause to learn" and nearly always refers to the teaching of the Scripture. You teach others by looking into God's Word together, allowing them to see you apply God's Word to your own life, and helping them grow in the knowledge and application of God's Word (Prov. 31:26).

Discipleship occurs many different ways. With our unique helper design, we have a special mandate to disciple younger women and guide them toward spiritual maturity (Titus 2:3-5). This is an area where older women in the church must reclaim ground. Those who are fighting against God's kingdom are spending an unreal amount of time, money, and energy to reproduce disciples. They have causes, we have a King! They have temporal hope, we have eternal promises! Here are a few ways discipleship can occur:

> In your key everyday relationships you have the opportunity to help others see Jesus and grow to be like Him.

Personal Discipleship: In your key everyday relationships you have the opportunity to help others see Jesus and grow to be like Him. This is the kind of life-on-life discipleship that occurs when you do more than just attend church on Sunday. This discipleship takes place as you live your life as an act of worship to the King. Through your family ties and friendships, you disciple. When you engage with others formally and informally to model and teach in order to further the Kingdom of God in the hearts and lives of those around you, you are discipling. If you are married, you disciple your husband. If you are a parent, you disciple your children. In such cases you don't need to do something more; you simply need to intentionally walk out your faith as an overflow of your own worship of Christ.

> **Do you have as your goal to help move those closest to you around the discipleship wheel? If so, how do you see this happening? If not, what would need to change?**

Process Discipleship: There are seasons of life where discipleship is particularly beneficial: through singleness, through being newly married or being a new mother, or some other life cycle or season. During these seasons, women often need more teaching and training to understand God's Word and more encouragement to follow His ways. New believers, like babies, especially need to be fed and taught how to feed themselves. They need instruction on spiritual disciplines and how to live out the rule of love in every area of life and every relationship. This type of discipleship might include regular meeting times for study, prayer, and accountability. These are all examples of seeing discipleship as part of a process of helping others grow and mature in Christ.

> **Is there anyone God has put in your life who would benefit from spending some structured instruction time with you?**

Problem-Solving Discipleship: The trials and temptations of life provide significant opportunities for growth. Think about your own life. When have you experienced the greatest "felt need" for Christ and change? People in trouble need the hope and help found in Christ. The more you receive comfort from His Word and learn how to apply that to yourself, the better prepared you will be to comfort others in their time of need and to help them grow in humility and dependence on Him (2 Cor. 1:3-11). The Bible tells Christians to gently restore those entangled in sin so that they will not be hardened by sin's deceitfulness and be rendered ineffective and unproductive in their knowledge of Christ (Gal. 6:1, Heb. 3:13, 2 Pet. 1:8). Jesus is the Prince of Peace and the Wonderful Counselor, but He has commissioned you to represent Him by bringing the message of peace and counsel to others through His Word (2 Tim 3:16-17).

> **Is there someone in your life who is struggling and needs the hope and help that Jesus provides? What promises of Scripture could you share for comfort? What commands of Scripture could you share for instruction? Remember that praying for and walking with those who are hurting are vital components of Christ-like counsel.**

Thy Kingdom Come!

In Matthew 6, Jesus teaches his disciples to pray through what Christians call the Lord's Prayer. His prayer includes these words: ***"Your kingdom come, your will be done, on earth as it is in heaven."*** (Matt. 6:10). When Jesus returns to earth, He won't come as suffering servant but as the conquering king (Rev. 19). He will set up His rule on earth as it is in heaven. How? All those who have trusted Christ throughout all generations will finally be free of the presence of sin, both inwardly and outwardly and will finally be free to worship Him perfectly. As you answer His call to multiply worshipers, you become a part of His kingdom coming on earth, and you can look forward to an eternity of worshiping Him together with those believers.

"THE KINGDOM LIFE" CHAPTER REVIEW

What doctrinal concepts were new or reinforced for you in this section?

SELF-COUNSEL JOURNAL

Read the Journal Instructions and the Journal Samples for help. (You can also find additional help and blank journal pages at knownministries.org.)

Complete the Self-Counsel Journal to connect your current struggle to how you REPRODUCE for the Kingdom.

Rule   Relate   Reflect   Represent   Reproduce   Restore   Repeat

REPRODUCE
Self-Counsel Journal Sample
Diane's Story

You may think that since Diane is relocating it will be difficult to be able to make disciples before she gets to know people. However, in her self-counsel journal she recognizes that in this season her disciple making efforts will be focused towards her family.

Reproduce: Multiplying Worshipers—Am I multiplying myself as a worshiper of God?

No. I have the opportunity to show my children, as well as others, that God's will for my life is the most important thing in my life. I have the opportunity to show them what it looks like to walk in cheerful obedience, but I have not consistently modeled this for them because I've had a worshiping problem—worshiping my selfish desires over God.

Am I worshiping Christ by imitating Him and showing Him as valuable in this situation?

In Luke 9, Jesus tells his followers that following him will cost them. He says, "Foxes have holes, and birds of the air have nests, but the Son of Man has nowhere to lay his head." His followers then begin to make excuses or conditions for following Christ. I'm afraid that much of these past few months, I have spent imitating those "followers" and not imitating Christ.

In this struggle how have I neglected my call to multiply worshipers?

Because obedience is an act of worship, and I have worshiped my own idea of comfort and security over God, I have sent the message that my idols deserve worship over Christ.

How can I use my struggle to share Christ with an unbeliever or encourage a believer?

The walk of faith is difficult and requires a constant dying to myself. We fail, but God's mercies are new every day, and forgiveness is always available through Christ. Our failures are always a beautiful opportunity to share the beauty of the Gospel.

How can I move the person along the discipleship wheel? What is their next step and how can I help them draw closer to God? Is God calling me to a specific type of discipleship in this situation?

In this situation, I need to speak Truth out loud to my daughter to combat the lies. I need to model for her (and for myself) that God is faithful and trustworthy.

REPRODUCE
Self-Counsel Journal
Rule: God as King—*Am I living under the absolute rule of the Most High King of the Universe in my heart and life?*

Relate: God as Father—*Am I relating to God as a beloved daughter with all the access and privilege my Father has bestowed on me?*

Reflect: Made in His Image—*Am I glorifying God by reflecting Him as a redeemed image bearer?*

Represent: Made by His Design—*Am I helping God as essential ally?*

Reproduce: Multiplying Worshipers—*Am I multiplying myself as a worshiper of God?*

1. Am I worshiping Christ by imitating Him and showing Him as valuable in this situation?

2. In this struggle how have I neglected my call to multiply worshipers?

3. How can I use my struggle to share Christ with an unbeliever or encourage a believer?

4. How can I move the person along the discipleship wheel? What is the next step for drawing that person closer to God?

5. Is God calling me to a specific type of discipleship in this situation?

NOTES

Rule   Relate   Reflect   Represent   Reproduce   Restore   Repeat

CHAPTER 5
RESTORE: MADE TO BEAUTIFY

1. Read the chapter and prayerfully answer the questions throughout the study to consider the truth of Representing God as a helper.

2. Use The Kingdom Life Chapter Review to reflect on the doctrinal truths that are new or reinforced.

3. Use the Self-Counsel Journal to continue to write about RULE, RELATE, REFLECT, REPRESENT, and REPRODUCE. Now add RESTORE to each journal entry. Do as many journal entries as you have need and time. You can copy the journal pages or print more at the website. (See the journal instructions in the Journal Introduction and the sample Self Counsel Journal, Diane's Story, for help. For additional help and examples go to knownministries.org.)

4. If you are meeting with a friend(s), use the Group Discussion Questions in Appendix II.

CHAPTER SIX

RESTORE: MADE TO BEAUTIFY

Scripture: Genesis 1 & 2

And God blessed them. And God said to them, "Be fruitful and multiply and fill the earth and subdue it, and have dominion over the fish of the sea and over the birds of the heavens and over every living thing that moves on the earth." (Genesis 1:28)

The LORD God took the man and put him in the garden of Eden to work it and keep it. (Genesis 2:15)

Jesus, Ultimate Beauty

Are you beginning to get excited about your part in God's Kingdom? Are you amazed that your King and Father would allow you to be a part of His mission in the lives of others? In order to multiply worshipers, you must live a life that shows Christ is your highest treasure. That might seem hard to do when your life seems to consist of everyday, ordinary tasks. The second part of God's mission for Adam and Eve—beautify—gives insight into how you can live every part of your life as an act of worship.

Before delving into what it means to beautify, it helps to understand what beauty really is. Last year Americans spent over thirteen billion dollars on improving their appearance. Could it be that the quest for physical beauty has only diminished our understanding of true beauty? The ancients understood that for something to be beautiful it must also be true and good and real. They believed that these four "transcendentals" (beauty, truth, goodness and realness) were bound together in such a way that something could not be one without being all four. With that idea in mind you can see that the bar for true beauty is extremely high and actually unattainable for any human. Only our King is truly beautiful. He alone is the Ultimate Beauty: beautiful, true, good and real. Scripture celebrates Jesus as the Beautiful One when it describes Him as the "radiance of God's glory" (Heb. 1:3).

Now, here's the good news: every believer, no matter how old, how styled, or what size you are, is pronounced beautiful in Christ. Theologian Al Mohler says, "Beauty is achieved when the thing created most closely and most perfectly glorifies its Creator." You can save all that money you spend on beauty supplies, because as you grow to look more like Jesus in the process of sanctification, you actually become more beautiful! You can be free from the obsession that the rest of the culture has with appearance and focus on the beauty of Christ. The Bible says that as you gaze on His beauty and stand in awe of Him you become more like Him, truly beautiful (2 Cor. 3:18).

> The Bible says that as you gaze on His beauty and stand in awe of Him you become more like Him, truly beautiful (2 Cor. 3:18).

You can see that what our culture calls beautiful is merely pretty or attractive. Certainly some things are attractive and beautiful, but many things are attractive and not beautiful. Dr. Mohler illustrates with this story:

I was approached some time ago by a young minister—a new pastor—who made a call upon an elderly lady who was in the hospital. Being like so many young pastors, as all of us who have been in that position can well remember, he was confronted with someone who needed more than he knew how to give. This elderly church member turned to him from her hospital bed and said, "Am I pretty?" He told me, "I lied and said 'Yes.'" The woman was suffering in the last stages of a degenerative disease, and she wasn't pretty. So that pastor's answer was probably the wrong one. I understood his heart, but I told him, "You need to change **pretty** to **beautiful**. This isn't pretty, but it is beautiful. [4]

---

4 Al Mohler, "A Christian Vision of Beauty, Part III, https://albert-mohler.com/2005/11/18/a-christian-vision-of-beauty-part-three.

Dr. Mohler recognized that while this elderly saint was outwardly decaying, she was actively being made to be more like Christ by the grace of God. She was becoming more beautiful with each passing day as she more closely resembled Christ.

> When we don't define beauty like God does we become discontent chasing what is pretty and fleeting: a better body, no wrinkles, the latest fashions, an immaculate home, and on and on. How much time do you spend each day on chasing what is merely pretty? How does your new understanding of beauty change your priorities?

Beauty in the Ordinary

You may be wondering, "Who has time to think about being beautiful? I'm happy if I have a clean shirt to put on!" Just about the time you feel like you have accomplished something, you realize that it needs to be done again. You do the laundry only to see the basket is full again. You go to work only to find your boss needs another report. You resolve a conflict only to find that you are caught in a new misunderstanding. You find it challenging to live "on mission" in the kingdom of God when so much of life seems chaotic. You long to live above the ordinary, fighting for a big mission where you partner with God to multiply worshipers of the King, but you find yourself overwhelmed by keeping the toilets clean! Understanding the beautify aspect of your mission will help you to see beyond the repetitive and unruly to the eternal significance of even the most ordinary tasks and everyday relationships.

> Name one area in your life that is ordinary and unruly (especially an area that frustrates you)?
> What about this area causes so much frustration?

Beautify Defined

If you are looking for the word "beautify" in Genesis, you won't find it. We use the term "beautify" to encompass the two commands God gave to Adam and Eve: to subdue the earth (Gen. 1:28) and to tend and keep the garden (Gen. 2:15). Many scholars believe that the Garden of Eden was cultivated, while the rest of the earth was not. The Garden serves as a model for the work Adam and Eve had to do on the rest of the earth. So, what was that work? Subdue, tend, and keep. Examining these three words can give you an idea of the rest of Adam and Eve's mission and yours, too.

- To subdue means to bring under control.
- To tend is to cultivate, which means to improve or develop by careful attention (**Webster's** online).
- To keep means to preserve something in its original state or in good condition and to protect it (**Webster's** online).

Putting these words together allows a definition of beautify to emerge. To "beautify" means to bring order to what is unruly or chaotic and to preserve it in the improved condition. When God gave mankind dominion over the earth, He expected His people to continue the work He began. God the Creator fashioned the earth and all that is in it out of nothing. As His agents, mankind reflects Him by producing things out of what He has already created. Simply put, He makes trees; humans make paper. In addition to creating, God the Father sustains all of His creation. He keeps it all going. The Bible says, *"He upholds the universe by the word of His power"* (Heb. 1:3, ESV). Mankind partners with God by cultivating and preserving the earth and all that is in it.

> To "beautify" means to bring order to what is unruly or chaotic and to preserve it in the improved condition.

Jesus came as the Great Beautifier. He left the perfection of heaven to enter into the darkness and chaos of our sin-saturated world. When John the Baptist is in prison feeling disillusioned and confused, he asks Jesus if He really is the Messiah. Jesus answers, *"Go and tell John what you see and hear. The blind receive their sight and the lame walk, lepers are cleansed and the deaf hear, and the dead are raised up, and the poor have good news preached to them"* (Matt. 11:4-5). What message does Jesus convey? He's saying that He is the Messiah, the One they prophesied about. Who else could reverse the curse and bring order out of chaos but the Messiah? He proved He was the Great Beautifier when He took on all that was evil and ugly, becoming sin on the cross, in order to save us from hell. The Beautiful One became infinitely ugly so that you could become beautiful again. When you become His child, you are declared beautiful and perfect before the Father, and as you grow to see Him and be more like Him you become even more beautiful. When you become like Jesus you not only multiply worshipers like He did, you also beautify, bring order out of chaos, like He did.

Jesus MADE you beautiful at the point of your salvation, and His Holy Spirit works to make you BECOME more beautiful as you grow to look like Jesus. In what area of your life have you come to see Him more clearly and become more like Him?

Beautifying Takes Work

You might be thinking, "Bringing order to chaos and preserving that order sounds like a lot of work! I can't even keep my pantry organized!" Yes, beautifying is work, but work is not a byproduct of the fall. The fall did have devastating effects on the jobs that God gave to mankind. Prior to the fall, the land would yield to Adam and Eve's efforts to beautify. After the fall, thorns and thistles would serve as a visible reminder of rebellion against the king. Another result of the Fall is that the world is constantly moving towards decay and disorder. You can see that all around you. Decay and disorder may seem to be silent invaders, taking over your home, your job, and your relationships. So how is this encouraging? This might seem strange, but knowing that sin makes your work difficult may bring a little bit of comfort. If you are like many women, you spend a lot of time trying to figure out why you feel so tired and overwhelmed. You may have to fight the temptation to frantically take control of everything around you or passively give up and check out. Genesis makes it clear: you are in a battle. You are fighting each day to push back the darkness all around you. You should be tired!

Just like a midwife has to continue to give the laboring mom the big picture in order to help her push through the pain, this new perspective may help you open your mind to see your seemingly small life in a totally different way. You are not simply doing mundane, repetitive tasks that quickly fall back into disorder; you are fulfilling your God-given image and design to beautify the world! You are an agent of the King. Pastor Tim Keller, says,

> . . . whenever we bring order out of chaos, whenever we draw out creative potential, whenever we elaborate and 'unfold' creation further than where it was when we found it —we are continuing God's work of creative, cultural development. Just as He "subdued" the earth in His work of creation, so He calls us now to labor as His representatives in a continuation and extension of that work.

As you labor here on earth as Christ's representative, you are a part of His kingdom coming here on earth just like it says in the Lord's Prayer: "Our Father, who art in heaven, hallowed be thy name. Your kingdom come, your will be done, on earth as it is in heaven" (Matthew 6:9-10, KJV). As you hallow God's name, His kingdom rule takes over your heart. That kingdom rule moves outward as you do His will here on earth as His agent. And you demonstrate that kingdom rule coming to the world as you restore order around you.

Reflect on your last few days. Make a list of all the ways you can identify where you are practicing the principles of beautify.

Beauty Operator

For as long as anyone can remember, my husband's grand-mother has gone each week to have her hair cut, set, and styled by her "beauty operator." Mimi has never called her a hairdresser. She is a beauty operator. And so are you! God uniquely made you as His agent, and He specifically gifted you and then placed you in a particular context in order to be His beauty operator. You are not armed with combs and scissors, but with God's Word, His Spirit, and His people. You can fight against what is unruly and chaotic to bring and sustain order. You can use all the resources He has given you to see your people and your community grow and flourish for the glory of God!

Where do you begin this work of beautifying? Start with the place you see the disorder and decay most clearly. Maybe it is your home. Your home provides endless examples of what is unruly and chaotic: laundry, yard work, the moldy produce bin in the refrigerator—and don't even start on the dust. Where does it come from? If you can lift your eyes from the dust bunnies for just a moment you will begin to see other areas of your life where you can be an agent of beauty: your work, your conversations, your relationships, your communi-ties, and more. Remember you are on a mission to beautify, to bring order to what is unruly or chaotic and to preserve it in the improved condition. Here are a few examples to consider as you think about your own life:

- A seamstress takes fabric and makes clothing
- An engineer designs system to harness energy and uses them for electricity
- A teacher takes unformed minds and shapes them with ideas
- An artist takes raw materials like paint, canvas, or clay to make works of art
- A musician takes tones and pitches to make beautiful music
- An architect and builder take pencil, paper, steel, wood, and concrete to create buildings and cities
- A wife takes the raw ingredients of food and makes them into a delicious meal

You can also bring order out of what is chaotic and unruly in relationships:

- A mother takes words and sentences and uses them to build encouragement for another mother or speak strength into her child

- A woman takes arguments and ideas and arranges them to bring peace out of conflict

- A wise friend sees struggle in another's heart and gently shows her the comfort and call of the gospel

- A woman looks at her past in order to gain understanding and to shine the light of truth on her shaping influences and beliefs

As you go about your daily life, ask yourself how God might be calling you to bring order, preserve order, or push back the darkness around you.

Beauty Restored

Even your simplest tasks can be consecrated to Him and elevated as valuable in the Kingdom. You cannot measure your success by how long it takes for your work to slide back into chaos, because that is happening constantly. You measure your success by how faithfully you do your work as unto the Lord (Col. 3:23). As you fight to push back the darkness, you can look forward to the day when you will work on the new earth without the constant fight against disorder and decay. The apostle Paul writes,

> *"For the creation waits with eager longing for the revealing of the sons of God. For the creation was subjected to futility, not willingly, but because of him who subjected it, in hope that the creation itself will be set free from its bondage to corruption and obtain the freedom of the glory of the children of God. For we know that the whole creation has been groaning together in the pains of childbirth until now. And not only the creation, but we ourselves, who have the firstfruits of the Spirit, groan inwardly as we*

> As you fight to push back the darkness, you can look forward to the day when you will work on the new earth without the constant fight against disorder and decay.

wait eagerly for adoption as sons, the redemption of our bodies. For in this hope we were saved. Now hope that is seen is not hope. For who hopes for what he sees? But if we hope for what we do not see, we wait for it with patience" (Rom. 8:19–25).

That is an incredible hope and worth the wait! There will be no more sorrow, pain or death (Rev. 21:4). In heaven, there will be pleasures so wonderful that your greatest earthly pleasures are only shadows of things to come (Ps.16:11). When Christ returns, His perfect kingdom will be restored on the New Heavens and New Earth (Rev. 21). Then, God's children will once again live in God's place under the loving rule of their heavenly Father for all eternity.

Can you imagine a world without sin? Can you imagine no poverty, decay, sickness, broken relationships, crime, addiction, pride, selfishness, anger? As you go about your life the next few days, think about how your world would look different without the presence of sin and the fall of humanity. Then, as you get a small glimpse of the glories of heaven, thank your heavenly Father for His great and precious promises to you through Christ!

"THE KINGDOM LIFE" CHAPTER REVIEW

What doctrinal concepts taught in this chapter were new to you or reinforced for you in this section?

Read the Journal Instructions and the Journal Samples for help. (You can also find additional help and blank journal pages at knownministries.org.)

Complete the Self-Counsel Journal to connect your current struggle to how you RESTORE for the Kingdom.

Rule   Relate   Reflect   Represent   Reproduce   Restore   Repeat

RESTORE
Self-Counsel Journal Sample
Diane's Story

Diane has many tasks around her home that will help to bring order to chaos. In this journal she challenges herself to focus on beautifying her heart and life spiritually as well.

Restore: Beautifying His World—Am I bringing order to what is unruly or chaotic and preserving it in the improved condition?

In a very tangible sense, I am working on improving an unruly, chaotic house that has not been updated or preserved. While it is very hard work, it is so much fun and rewarding to see the fruit of my labor. While I am tempted to bemoan that I won't be able to enjoy the home that I've put all of this work into, I am trying to pray for and give thanks for those who will love this home after us and I pray that they will continue to preserve this home's beauty and character.

1. Have I neglected any God-given responsibilities during this struggle?

Knowing that I am moving, I have been tempted to go ahead and withdraw from community, church, neighbors, etc. I've been tempted to neglect investing myself in others.

2. What tasks are you viewing as too small to be beneficial to the kingdom?

3. What chaos do you see in your environment, your relationships or your own thinking that can be brought into God's order?

While most of my time and energy have been spent putting order in my house so that we can sell it, I need to focus more energy on righting the spiritual ship in my own heart and in my home. My family is in transition with my husband gone during the week. My son misses his dad and feels some insecurity while he's gone. My daughter worries about what the future holds. My husband feels bad for being gone and for causing all of this change. My own emotions swing wildly depending on the day and the circumstances. I need to spend as much time and energy on my family that I am spending on my house. My house got in the shape it's in because it was neglected. I don't want the same to happen to my marriage or my family.

4. What are some practical steps you can take to bring order around you?

I need to be sure to spend regular time in God's Word and prayer. When I sense that my emotions are taking over and crowding out what I know to be true, I need to spend more time focusing on the truth, asking the Lord to search my heart and root out sin, repenting and worshipping Him rightly. Then I need to be more intentional about assessing how I can encourage those around me with the truth of His Word.

5. What have you taken dominion over when God has not given you dominion in that place?

my plans for the future

REPRODUCE
Self-Counsel Journal

Chapter 1 Rule: God as King—*Am I living under the absolute rule of the Most High King of the universe in my heart and life?*

Chapter 2 Relate: God as Father—*Am I relating to God as a beloved daughter with all the access and privilege my Father has bestowed on me?*

Chapter 3 Reflect: Made in His Image—*Am I glorifying God by reflecting Him as a redeemed image bearer?*

Chapter 4 Represent: Made by His Design—*Am I helping God as His essential ally?*

Chapter 5 Reproduce: Made to Multiply—*Am I multiplying myself as a worshiper of God?*

Chapter 6 Restore: Made to Beautify—*Am I bringing order to what is unruly or chaotic and preserving it in the improved condition?*

1. Have I neglected any God-given responsibilities during this struggle?

2. What tasks am I viewing as too small to be beneficial to the kingdom?

3. What chaos do I see in my environment, my relationships, or my own thinking that can be brought into God's order?

4. What are some practical steps I can take to bring order around me?

5. What have I taken dominion over when God has not given me dominion in that place?

NOTES

CHAPTER SEVEN

REPEAT:
THE MISSION

We fervently pray that you will not close this book and put it on the shelf with so many others. The process of learning to trust and obey God in our trials is lifelong. The beginning of each trial is an invitation to seek Him. Oftentimes, God allows our struggles to continue so that we will return to Him over and over again deepening our intimacy with Him. While we most often desire to be out of our struggle, God desires most for us to know His unfathomable love for us in the trial. We pray this tool will continue to be used and useful in your sanctification toolbox. We long for you to actively pursue God and have His kingdom come to rule in your life to bring glory to Him.

We challenge you to take other women through this material and to share with them what you have learned. This "one another revolution" starts with you and me, but it does not end here! Jesus intends to use us to reach the world for Him and build His kingdom until He returns. Will you be faithful to the call? Will you join us as we seek deeper worship and more worshipers for our great God and king?

> Write down the names of several women in your sphere of influence whom you could pray about inviting to meet with you. To whom do you have natural access? For starters, you have your neighbors, coworkers, daughters, church members, or other people who regularly engage with in your community. Begin praying the Lord will give you an opportunity to invite these women to meet with you.

Rule Relate Reflect Represent Reproduce Restore Repeat

After prayerful consideration:

1. Decide whom will you invite. We often say, "All you have to do is be willing and show up; God will do the rest." It can be intimidating to ask someone to study the Bible with you. What if they say "no"? My husband would say, "Ask anyway. You had a "no" when you got up this morning!" In other words, everyone you don't ask is a NO, so go ahead and ask. It is not up to you to determine who will come. Just be faithful to make the invitation and pray God will draw women to you, even one! And keep asking until someone says, "yes".

2. Decide where you will meet. One of your greatest resources is your home. An open door is an open invitation into your life. If your home is not an option, get creative. You can meet in a coffee shop, playground, park, or even online (video chatting works great). If you work outside your home, can you meet during lunch at your office, a park, or local diner?

3. Decide when you will meet. Your meeting time is going to be dictated by your availability and the availability of the women you engage. Pick a time that is best for you and consider scheduling conflicts as God's way of directing who needs to be in your group.

4. Decide how long you will meet. The study is going to be 7–8 weeks depending on how you break it up. Pick a date to begin. You could meet the first night and have personal introductions (we suggest preparing a few questions for everyone to answer), hand out the study, explain the study format, and take prayer requests. Then you will have seven weeks to complete the study. We suggest you have a definite start and end time, sixty to ninety minutes should be sufficient.

5. Decide if you will ask for a commitment. We recommend laying out all the details and expectations at the beginning and asking for a commitment. In our experience, women open up and share more deeply in an environment where consistency and accountability are present.

If you would like, please let us know you are engaged in this study by posting on our social media on Instagram or Facebook at KNOWN ministries. We would be so encouraged to see pictures of you and of the women you are engaging with.

Finally, don't feel like you have to have all the answers to everyone's questions. You are still a disciple even as you are making disciples! If you have any questions or concerns, feel free to reach out to us at **knownministries.org** or **alex@ knownministries.org** or **brenda@knownministries.org.** We will do our best to help you or point you in the right direction! God's richest blessing to you. And thank you for joining the "One Another Revolution"!

SELF-COUNSEL JOURNAL INSTRUCTIONS

God's desire is for you to continually live under His loving rule as His daughter in order to be transformed by Him and to glorify Him. Each day you encounter trials and temptations that tempt you to pledge your allegiance to another ruler and forget His goodness and your purpose. Use this journal regularly (even daily) as a way to reorient yourself to the King and His kingdom and to align your life with His loving rule. **Journaling is vital to gaining the full benefit of this study. You will use your journals as you work through each chapter to apply what you are learning to daily life!**

Please notice that in every journaling response there are at least five components:

- **Honesty.** God really cares about your struggles. Run to Him and pour out your heart before Him.

- **Confession.** Look at what you wrote down. Ask the Holy Spirit to show you where your thinking and believing are wrong or your hoping and trusting is misplaced. Simply confess it as sin and ask for forgiveness.

- **Thankfulness.** Jesus is the key who opens all God's blessings to His children. Forgiveness should lead you to worship. Believe you are fully forgiven every time and bow your heart to Him in gratitude.

- **Repentance.** Repent just means to turn from your sin and turn to God in faith and obedience. You cannot change apart from the Holy Spirit who gives you the desire and power to change. Take hold of Him by faith and cling to Him for real and lasting change that pleases God.

- **Repetition.** You are only seeing one journal entry on one specific struggle. You can use this journal over and over again as you go deeper into one struggle or as you encounter other trials. The book of James says that perseverance is necessary for spiritual growth. Don't give up! The journal is a meditation tool to see more of His glorious grace through the prism of your problems.

Self-Counsel Journal Question Prompts

Chapter 1. Rule: God as King—*Am I living under the absolute rule of the Most High King of the universe in my heart and life?*

1. Who or what is ruling my heart? (Whoever or whatever rules you controls you.) Who or what is competing for God's rule in my life?

2. Am I challenging God's right to rule in my life? How can I counsel myself to trust His rule?

3. How does God's holiness (the perfection of all His attributes) comfort me? What attribute of God is especially meaningful for me now? What would change if I embraced this attribute?

4. How does the sovereignty of God (His absolute rule over the universe) comfort me? How does it trouble me? How should it challenge my current thinking?

5. How is Satan undermining God's rule in my life by attacking the truths of God's Word and His character?

6. How does the hope of God's future reign help me in my current circumstances?

Chapter 2 Relate: God as Father—*Am I relating to God as a beloved daughter with all the access and privilege my Father has bestowed on me?*

1. How does access to God as my Father change the way I handle my sin or suffering?

2. How does reflecting on God's wisdom and goodness at the cross help me in my current struggle?

3. Am I living as if the penalty of sin has been paid? I am forgiven!

4. Am I living as if the power of sin has been broken? I can obey!

5. Am I living in light of the fact that the presence of sin will be removed? This will end!

Chapter 3 Reflect: Made in His Image—*Am I glorifying God by reflecting Him as a redeemed image bearer?*

1. In what ways am I striving to **be** God, instead of being **like** God?

2. Am I placing value on what God says is valuable, or am I allowing someone or something else to define worth?

3. Have I rightly understood the depth of my sinfulness due to image distortion?

4. In what ways have I made God in my image, believing lies and distortions about Him?

5. How can I reflect God's worth, weight, and renown as I struggle with my sin/suffering?

6. How can I depend on the Holy Spirit, God's Word, and other Christians for. . . ?

7. How am I rejoicing in the good God is producing in my circumstance (Christ-likeness), knowing this is His ultimate goal for me?

Chapter 4 Represent: Made by His Design—*Am I helping God as His essential ally?*

1. Where am I being tempted to abandon my job as an essential ally?

2. Am I helping or working against God?

3. What deficits do I see? How am I being critical or complaining? How would help come through me?

4. Am I comparing myself to others? How is this hurting my ability to help?

5. Am I creating or alleviating suffering? What needs to change for others to say, "Life without her is suffering."

Chapter 5 Reproduce: Made to Multiply—*Am I multiplying myself as a worshiper of God?*

1. Am I worshiping Christ by imitating Him and showing Him as valuable in this situation?

2. In this struggle, how have I neglected my call to multiply worshipers?

3. How can I use my struggle to share Christ with an unbeliever or encourage a believer?

4. How can I move the person along the discipleship wheel? What is their next step and how can I help them draw closer to God?

5. Is God calling me to a specific type of discipleship in this situation?

Chapter 6 Restore: Made to Beautify—*Am I bringing order to what is unruly or chaotic and preserving it in the improved condition?*

1. Have I neglected any God-given responsibilities during this struggle?

2. What tasks am I viewing as too small to be beneficial to the kingdom?

3. What chaos do I see in my environment, my relationships, or my own thinking that can be brought into God's order?

4. What are some practical steps I can take to bring order around you?

5. What have I taken dominion over when God has not given me dominion in that place?

Simple 6 R's Self-Counsel Journal

Rule: God as King—*Am I living under the absolute rule of the most high king of the universe in my heart and life?*

Relate: God as Father—*Am I relating to God as a beloved daughter with all the access and privilege my Father has bestowed on me?*

Reflect: Made in His Image—*Am I glorifying God by reflecting Him as a redeemed image bearer?*

Represent: Made by His Design—*Am I helping God as essential ally?*

Reproduce: Made to Multiply—*Am I multiplying myself as a worshiper of God?*

Restore: Made to Beautify—*Am I bringing order to what is unruly or chaotic and preserving it in the improved condition?*

GROUP DISCUSSION QUESTIONS

RULE: God as King

1. Look back over the different ways people approach Scripture and consider what the outcome might be when approaching it in different ways. Why do you think considering the Bible as a story is important for your daily life?

2. Name something about God's qualifications to rule—His holiness? In what ways do you struggle to be like God instead of acknowledging your limits and trusting in Him?

3. In what circumstance in your life or the world does God's sovereignty comfort you? In what ways does it trouble you?

4. Exercise or small group question at the end: Describe a time your eyes were open to evil and the impact it had on you? (It might be a movie, an awful personal experience, the knowledge of some evil in the world, etc.)

5. Using your sanctified imagination and what you know from God's Word about His loving rule, discuss how you imagine life when the King returns. Take a few minutes to pray and praise God together. When you get the King, you get the Kingdom!

RELATE: God as Father

1. How is the glory of God made more manifest through the Fall of Adam and Eve? What attributes of God are displayed as a result of the Fall that might not otherwise have been put on display?

2. Have you used or heard Romans 8:28 quoted? How does this view of God's goodness challenge your current thinking?

3. As His daughter, what does access to the King mean for you when you sin? What does it mean for you when you suffer?

4. When you considered the penalty Christ paid to give you access to the Father, what was your reaction? How can you better appreciate the hell He endured, so you won't have to?

5. Your access to the Father is experienced through prayer. Can you put into words what it will be like to have full and complete access to Him at all times?

REFLECT: Made in His Image

1. What are some ways that you "reflect" God's image in current relationships and responsibilities?

2. Which people in your life do you struggle to view as valuable image bearers? Why do you think it is difficult?

3. How do women devalue themselves as image bearers? How does the culture devalue women as image bearers?

4. If you are single, how can your life be one of more focused devotion to Christ?

5. Can you think of a time in your life when your wrong view of God was corrected? How did it impact you?

6. When you look back on history or in our current age, how have you seen people become less human as they function under their own rule? How do people in turn dehumanize others when they don't follow God's rule?

REPRESENT: Made by His Design

1. Who has been the most influential person to shape your views about women? And how has this example/influence impacted you?

2. Is the idea of helper as a "design" versus a "role" new for you? If so, how does it change your thinking about women and their mission?

3. In what areas/ways do you find women struggle with criticism, comparison, and complaining that may be different than men? How would you use this lesson to help a woman struggling with criticism, comparison, or complaining?

4. What has been your experience as a woman in the culture, the church, and your family? What has been positive? What has been negative?

5. Name one area in your life where you believe if you were not involved than someone else would have suffered?

6. What do you think would change if the men in your world read and embraced this lesson?

REPRODUCE: Made to Multiply

1. Have you considered that Jesus is the first disciple maker? When you look at His discipling relationship and consider imitating Him what comes to mind?

2. How has your view of worship changed from this chapter?

3. Are you fearful to point non-Christians to Christ? If so, why? How does looking at more as a process through authentic relationship help you? Or, does it make you more uncomfortable and why?

4. In which of the different avenues for discipleship (personal, process, and problem-directed) do you find yourself most often engaged? What makes this one easy for you and the others more difficult?

5. How do you imagine the new heavens and earth will be with everyone able to worship Jesus perfectly?

RESTORE: Made to Beautify

1. If you think of the four transcendentals (beauty, truth, realness, and goodness), can you think of other things that reflect the true beauty of Christ?

2. How does this definition of beauty make you feel?

3. As you are made more beautiful, you in turn beautify your relationships and environment. How have you seen that happen in your life?

4. How does understanding your mission as twofold, multiply and beautify, help you see your priorities more clearly?

5. One day when Jesus returns again, God has promised to restore all that has been lost in the fall. Where do you personally most long to see restoration happen?

REPEAT: The Mission

1. Now that the study is complete, share your biggest takeaways. How are you different as a result of this study?

2. Discuss the idea of a "one another revolution" and your place in it. Where have you been a Warrior Woman by multiplying and beautifying? Where do you see God stretching you next?

3. As you consider leading another woman through material (or any study), what concerns do you have? What would it take to alleviate those concerns?

4. Take some time to end your study by praying your part in God's mission and the one another revolution!

Acknowledgments

We owe a huge thank you to many people for helping us get this study into your hands. Thank you to Mandy Kavanaugh for believing in us in the early days and helping get Known Ministries off the ground. Rick Steele and Noah Craig without your editing and formatting help, this would still be a file on our computers, thank you! Thank you to Deana Hodge and Laura Jones for providing invaluable feedback and support. Thank you to the many women at Young Meadows Presbyterian Church in Montgomery, Alabama and in Chattanooga, Tennessee, who allowed us to "test drive" this material in Sunday School classes, retreats, and Bible studies. We also appreciate Lauren Duncan who did our beautiful cover painting, "Job 37:5." You can find prints of this painting and see her other work at **laurenjohnstonduncan.com** or on Instagram **@artbyljd**. We thank our husbands. They thought pregnancy was long! Who knew it would take two years to birth this little baby!! Thank you for your patience and kindness to us and for your fierce support of all that we do. Are we ready for another one?!?! Most of all, thank you King Jesus for making us your daughters and giving us good work to do in Your kingdom. Come quickly, Lord!

About the Authors

ALEX KOCHER

ALEX KOCHER teaches, counsels, and mentors in order to see the kingdom of God advance through women who display the beauty of Christ. She currently works as the Women's Director at Young Meadows Presbyterian Church and as a certified biblical counselor. Although originally from the North, Alex moved to the South as fast as she could and received a Bachelor's degree in Elementary Education, with certifications in Special Education from Furman University and a Master's degree in School Psychometry from Troy University, Montgomery. She is a biblical counselor through the Association of Certified Biblical Counselors, and she has also completed the Level One certificate from the Christian Counseling and Education Foundation.

For the past several years, Alex has participated in Be the Bridge, Montgomery, a diverse group of women who are committed to gospel-driven dialogue about race issues. Alex is a founding member of KNOWN ministries which equips and trains women to be disciple-making disciples. She enjoys reading, teaching, and conference speaking. Alex has been married to her husband, Mason, who has been making her laugh for more than twenty-five years. They have two daughters who are convinced their parents live to embarrass them. Alex loves good friends, good food, and good conversation.

BRENDA PAYNE is passionate about inspiring, equipping and training women in the personal ministry of the Word and problem solving discipleship.

She was the first woman to be certified in the state of Alabama with the Association of Biblical Counselors where she ministered to women for more than twenty years. She is currently a "volunteer" for Jesus in her new hometown of Chattanooga, Tennessee, where she counsels and conducts lay counseling training. Brenda is completing her Master's of Biblical Counseling from Faith Seminary with an emphasis on training and helping families of addicts.

Brenda and her husband, Paul, enjoy hospitality, including managing their "Scenic City" Airbnb. They have three grown children, two of whom cheer "War Eagle!" Brenda is an "otter" who loves to be with people and have fun with friends!

Brenda worships and works at Calvary Chapel Chattanooga. She is the co-founder of Known Ministries and the Chattanooga Biblical Counseling and Discipleship Network. Brenda co-authored the *Teach Them Diligently* study guide and wrote *Motherhood: Hope for Discouraged Moms*. Brenda received her Bachelor's in Broadcast Journalism from Troy University and worked as a television news anchor and reporter in Dothan and Montgomery, Alabama.

BRENDA PAYNE

70458479R00063

Made in the USA
Columbia, SC
21 August 2019